D1263368

The

Garland

CLASSICS OF
FILM LITERATURE

REPRINTED IN PHOTO-FACSIMILE
IN 32 VOLUMES

The Private Life of Henry VIII

Lajos Biro

and

Arthur Wimperis

GARLAND PUBLISHING, INC. ● NEW YORK & LONDON ● 1978

Robert Manning Strozier Library

JUL 10 1978

Tallahassee, Florida

Reprinted by arrangement
with Eyre Methuen Ltd.

Library of Congress Cataloging in Publication Data

Biró, Lajos, 1880-1948.
  The private life of Henry VIII.

  (The Garland classics of film literature)
  Screenplay for the motion picture of the same name.
  Reprint of the 1934 ed. published by Methuen, London.
  1. Henry VIII, King of England, 1491-1547--Drama.
I. Wimperis, Arthur, 1874-1953, joint author.   II.   The
Private life of Henry VIII. [Motion picture] II. Series.
PN1997.P76 1977   791.43'7   76-52090
ISBN 0-8240-2866-X

Printed in the United States of America

THE PRIVATE LIFE OF
HENRY VIII

CHARLES LAUGHTON AS HENRY VIII

THE PRIVATE LIFE
OF HENRY VIII

Directed by
ALEXANDER KORDA

Story and Dialogue by
LAJOS BIRO
AND
ARTHUR WIMPERIS

Produced by
LONDON FILM PRODUCTIONS LTD.

Edited, with an Introduction, by
ERNEST BETTS

METHUEN & CO. LTD. *LONDON*
36 Essex Street W.C.

First published in 1934

PRINTED IN GREAT BRITAIN

THE PRODUCER

ALEXANDER KORDA

began as a newspaper reporter. Directed[1] films in 1916 in Budapest, and later went to Vienna, Rome, and Berlin, where he made pictures for the famous Ufa Company. Produced in Hollywood in 1926, joining the First National Film Company, for whom he made numerous pictures, including *The Stolen Bride*. Later joined the Fox Production Company before going back to First National for three years. One of his best-known pictures for this company was the *Private Life of Helen of Troy*. After being with Fox again in 1930, he left for Europe, and made several pictures for Paramount at their Paris (Joinville) studios.

His first British picture was *Service for Ladies*, which was acclaimed one of the best British films up to that time. In 1932 he formed his own film company, London Film Productions, and made that amusing satire on Mayfair marriages, *Wedding Rehearsal*, and *Men of To-morrow*, a story of Oxford life. The next film he directed was *The Girl from Maxims*. Then followed *The Private Life of Henry VIII* and *Catherine the Great*. *The Private Life of Don Juan*, with Douglas Fairbanks in the title role, was his next production, and his latest (1933) is *The Scarlet Pimpernel*, directed by Harold Young.

[1] The director of a film is the counterpart of the stage 'producer'. A 'producer' in the cinema is usually the supervisor of pictures, though he may also direct them, as in Mr. Korda's case.

THE AUTHORS

LAJOS BIRO

Hungarian, b. Vienna, 1880

has published, in Budapest, some thirty volumes of plays, novels, and short stories, many translated into German, Swedish, and other languages.

Plays presented in Europe and America include *The Tsarina* (with Melchior Lengyel), *The Moonflower, Yellow Lily, The Robber Knight, Hotel Imperial, Quadrille.*

Novels: *Woman Triumphant, The House of Molitor, Don Juan's Three Nights, The Jews of Bazin,* etc.

Four collections of short stories.

Has written numerous films, the chief of which are *The Last Command, The Way of all Flesh, Hotel Imperial, Service for Ladies, The Private Life of Henry VIII* and *Catherine the Great* (with Arthur Wimperis).

Mr. Biro began his career as a journalist and became reporter, dramatic critic, leader-writer, and war correspondent, in Budapest. Left Hungary after the war and lived in Rome, Paris, Berlin, and Hollywood, where he devoted himself principally to films.

ARTHUR WIMPERIS

b. London, 1876; *ed. Dulwich College*

dramatic author and lyrist. Wrote *lyrics* of *The Dairymaids, The Gay Gordons, The Arcadians,* etc.

Author of many 'Follies' burlesques, *The Girl in the Taxi* (with Frederick Fenn), *Within the Law, The Laughing Husband.*

Author of *The Passing Show.*

Author (with Hartley Carrick) of *M'mselle Tra-La-la, The Little Lamb, The Rajah's Ruby, By Jingo, Follow the Crowd.*

Wrote (with Basil Hood) *Bric-à-brac*; (with Max Pemberton): *My Lady Frayle, Vanity Fair, Pamela, The Shop Girl* (revised version), *Just Fancy*; *London, Paris and New York, The Curate's Egg*; (with Harry Vernon) *A Perfect Fit*; (with Ronald Jeans) *Still Dancing*; (with Lauri Wylie) *Princess Charming, A Warm Corner, Song of the Sea*, and a later adaptation of *A Warm Corner*.

Adaptation of *He's Mine*, and with Austin Melford, *Nippy* and *Lovely Lady*.

Mr. Wimperis has also adapted many plays from the French, including *The Trump Card, Bluebeard's Eighth Wife, The Return* and *The Elopement*, and from the German *Love and Laughter* and *Louis the Fourteenth*.

Films include *The Private Life of Henry VIII* (with Lajos Biro); *Catherine the Great, The Private Life of Don Juan*, and (in collaboration) *The Scarlet Pimpernel*.

INTRODUCTION

THIS is the first complete script of a British film to be published in book form. The text which follows reproduces exactly the scenes, dialogue, and technical details of *The Private Life of Henry VIII*, and—if it is not too wild a claim —introduces a new form of literature.

That no such attempt has yet been made is due to a number of causes. First, scarcely anything has been written, in this country at least, that was worth publishing. Secondly, there are those who say that the publication of a film is difficult to justify, since the more fully the written word appears on the screen the less satisfactory the subject will be as a motion-picture. Any hint of the literary or theatrical in a film is considered by screen purists a violation of 'true cinema', whatever that may be.

Such a belief can only be held of a particular class of film —the documentary, the abstract, the cartoon, and those art-and-crafty works which still entertain the specialized audiences of film societies and coteries. But in the meantime a film drama of increasing significance, to which well-known writers and artists are contributing, is growing up and is making its small but visible niche in literature.

Few people have any idea of the way a film is written or what it is like to read. In manuscript, it reads very like a play. The technical details are different, consisting of highly specialized directions for lighting, camera work, sets, and so forth. There are no 'acts'; the film is reduced to reels (generally seven or eight) and to an infinite number of sequences, scenes, or shots. But the interiors or backgrounds are described as a dramatist would describe them, with perhaps more detail and a terminology of hilarious aspect to the average reader. The dialogue, though more economical and active, resembles that of a play.

As the cinema exists at present, a film has no life, either for the 'author', the director, or the public, beyond its transitory appearance on the screen. The author of a film is still the most despised of men, and the director fares very little better. He is a success if he does what he is told and pawns his future to an immediate popularity.

I was discussing this point with Mr. Alfred Hitchcock one day after the presentation of one of his films—I think it was *Murder*, from Clemence Dane's novel, *Enter Sir John*. I asked him how he proposed to secure immortality in the cinema (if such a thing could be imagined), and whether he was satisfied that even the best screen drama, having been unwound to the public, was sufficient monument to its creator when it went into the tin can which was its final resting-place.

Mr. Hitchcock's answer was that he had no further interest in a film once he had put down every detail of it on paper. There was the film; he had, in imagination, created and made it already; the rest was a matter of mechanics, money, studio technique, and how far the leading lady consented to be led.

Mr. Hitchcock's view, I found, was held by many other film directors. Indeed, I have met few directors who did not consider the actual labour of rehearsal and production a prolonged and exasperating bore. To the director, the film was always more real on paper than it was on the screen, but the screen, of necessity, was its final and appropriate form.

One could apply the same argument to the stage. A play, in the eyes of its author, is complete as a piece of literature, when it is written, but it only fulfils the author's intention when it is staged. The stage gives it voice, life, and colour. And, indeed, if the writing of film plays had been taken more seriously, we should not have had to wait until now for their publication. Had the screen come into the world with the idea first instead of the machinery, there would have been a literature of the screen long ago—crude, no doubt, appalling to contemplate, but comparable, nevertheless, with the first faint scrawlings of the drama.

For some time after my talk with Mr. Hitchcock I waited in the hope of finding some film which would give as much pleasure to the general reader as it does to the director in scenario form. But pictures continued to be pictures without taste or imagination, and every good judge resented the literary intrusion.

When, in 1929, the talkies arrived and produced a huge crop of photographed plays, the situation changed, though very little for the better. The works of Thomas Hardy, J. M. Barrie, Eugene O'Neill, Sir Arthur Pinero, John Galsworthy, Frederick Lonsdale, Noël Coward, and others were bought up by the film producers for enormous sums, adopted by new parents, slaughtered or disembowelled, and re-born as the bastard creations of the Hollywood imagination. None of the authors seemed to take any interest in their works once the contract had been signed for their production as films.

But in the meantime the spoken word had entered—a serious and imposing word. It was a third dimension, a vital element in the film, which broadened its scope and renewed its life. It scared and antagonized many people, myself included, who saw the silent screen obscured by verbiage and the picture struck down in the act of taking breath to move.

Those of us who held that view have had to change our minds. The talkie having arrived was too powerful to resist; it was obviously a richer and more wonderful medium, and as a new dramatic instrument was welcomed by such pronounced talkie-haters as Pudovkin and Eisenstein, who have since used sound in their own non-theatrical ways for the propagandist film.

Film directors in Hollywood such as Charlie Chaplin, King Vidor, Lewis Milestone, Joseph Von Sternberg, and a few others, and in Europe such as René Clair, G. W. Pabst, Marcel L'Herbier, and Fritz Lang, fought for the

'freedom of the screen', but in most cases were over·
whelmed. None of these directors, by the way, could have
told you what they meant by 'freedom of the screen', and
had they done so the idea would have been regarded by
the studios as a mere academic brawl unrelated to the
primary object of the cinema, namely, the continuous piling
up of money. The idea of 'freedom' was something to
which the genuine film-maker clung jealously, as a child
clings to its toys. It was a mood of panic in a period of
revolution.

In a year or two, however, a cleavage occurred between
the film which was simply a photographed play and the
film which aimed, however feebly, at maintaining a balance
between the picture and the word. Ninety-eight per cent
of films were a jumble of words barking out American
wise-cracks to twenty million people a week in this country
and ninety million a week in America. So it is to-day;
and it would be foolish, I suppose, for any man to declare
that the talkie was not greatly entertaining, whatever he
might think of its artistry. Meanwhile, as most films were
adapted from books and plays, written by half a dozen
different writers, or not written at all, but produced, as
they say, 'on the cuff', their literary value was negligible.

When the writing was good, as in *What Price Hollywood?*,
Forbidden, or *Trouble in Paradise*, the fact was rarely recog-
nized, and the names of the writers were so extraordinary
that it was impossible to mention them in public without
roars of laughter. Some of the best Hollywood writers
have the oddest names—Zoë Akins (who wrote *The Greeks
Had a Word for It*), Jo Swerling, Samuel Spewack, Earl Derr
Biggers, Gertrude Tonkonogy and William Slavens McNutt.
Mrs. Trampleasure from the telephone book could hardly
do better.

Nevertheless, these are masters of their craft in the screen
literature of America. They are pioneers. They introduce
a new form of writing—a form which can best be described
as *writing to action*. To put words on the move: that is the

task of the screen writer capable of his job. As movement is the soul of drama, as well as of screen drama, you might have supposed that the dramatist would be first in the field as a screen writer. But dramatists have proved quite inadequate to the task, though one or two, such as Benn Levy, Reginald Berkeley, and Clemence Dane, have succeeded. But in the main they despised the work; and when, tempted by huge rewards, they tried it, they were shown to be dismally unconscious of the things demanded of them. The most successful dramatists have been those, like P. G. Wodehouse, who were alleged to have been paid for doing nothing at all. It was said of Emil Ludwig when he went not long ago to Hollywood that he was staggered at the idleness of screen writers who took a fortnight thinking of their subjects, five weeks writing them down, and a fortune the moment some other writer was asked to take on the job. Ludwig himself, I believe, produced a full script in five days.

Why is it, then, apart from these ancient abuses, that the reputable dramatist fights shy of writing direct for the screen? It is, first, because the screen lacks dramatic prestige; it does not count as an artistic medium; and secondly, because the literary artist who is offered, let us say, £5,000 to go to Hollywood, feels that the money, rather than the art, will determine the character of his work. He himself does not matter.

That is true. Only to-day is the convention breaking down. But it is also true that until the screen has a real interest for the general reader and the student, who absorb and appreciate it and give it their critical aid, it must remain a shadow on the screen without significance, or lie buried with a thousand other tinned dramas in the vaults of Wardour Street. (It is appalling to think that over fifteen thousand such films have been produced since 1915 and are now, thank Heaven! forgotten.)

It occurred to me, therefore, that it would be of value to the cinema to rescue some of the best films from oblivion.

For it is as great a pleasure to recall the films which gave us special enjoyment as it is to hear a song well recorded on the gramophone or to read a good talk heard on the wireless.

Until lately, however, there have been no talkies worth publishing. It was Mr. Lewis Milestone (director of *All Quiet on the Western Front*) who first put me in the way of one. Last year he planned a trip to Russia in order to make a film of Moscow and the Revolution. Naturally a writer of distinction joined him in the venture. He was Laurence Stallings, whose *What Price Glory?* shocked the film-goers of 1928 when they heard the oaths they had used in war-time blurted forth from the screen by Victor McLaglen and Edmund Lowe. Naturally, with Milestone and Stallings, was another author with an extraordinary name. He was Ilya Ehrenbourg, known to film-goers as the author of *The Loves of Jeanne Ney*, and to many more for his book *A Street in Moscow*. In 1922 he published a novel, *The Life and Death of Nicholas Kourbov*, and on this story the film was to be based.

While Mr. Milestone was away in Russia he lent me the script of his film. It was a brilliant piece of writing, impossible to lay aside once you had picked it up. Character and scene stood out in high relief and had such energy that the scenario seemed bent like an arrow and ready to fly from the screen. But above all it was good reading as well as good scenario. The background, copiously filled in and alive with conspiracy, had the excitement of a novel by Balzac, and the hordes of plotters, fanatics, degenerates, and aristocrats peopling the scene were so clearly realized that you could not doubt their authenticity.

The Red Square, as it was provisionally called, was never produced. It contained too much truth and was regarded by its sponsors, Columbia Pictures, as politically dangerous.

This script, nevertheless, a full 'shooting script' ready for the studio, persuaded me that there was a genuine literature of the screen, and that it was diverting enough to interest the general reader—more, that it might serve to convince the world that the cinema is not the inane bag of tricks of popular belief but a living word-picture of our time to refresh and renew mankind.

As to the form such a scenario should take, that is a point on which few are learned enough to dogmatize. There are no set forms in the cinema. What should be the form of a fall of rain or a gust of wind or of anything which expresses itself in perpetual motion? A number of films, silent and sound, which I choose arbitrarily—*The Italian Straw Hat, Entr'acte, Ballet Mécanique, Dr. Caligari, Waxworks, Destiny*, and many fine forgotten films of the German school; Flaherty's *Moana* and *Man of Aran*—are successful only because they dispense with formal dramatic rules, have no plot or character-drawing but merely fall into the camera lens in a pleasing pictorial order. Such efforts are in the highest degree filmic, since no consideration of drama, with its false economies of time and space, hinders the natural flow of images on the screen. The director is quite free to tell you, by his gift of selection and choice of material, what he finds significant in a picture, what is his attitude to life.

These specialized films, however, would be dull reading to the general public; they make a text-book for technicians and theorists. My object here is to interest a wider audience and make room for the popular film drama of our time, for it would be absurd to regard the cinema as anything but a popular medium of expression. It is a show which must stand the rough-and-tumble of the average man's judgment. There are films which fulfil that need and yet remain good film-craft. They are not 'pure movie', to use the undergraduate phrase of the *avant garde*, but they select with care the story, cast and director, the sounds, scenes, and speeches of which film plays are composed. They are well written, dramatic, and seasoned specimens of the talkie.

The Private Life of Henry VIII was a film of this order. It is good popular movie and it is good reading. It was directed by Alexander Korda in the face of universal discouragement and scepticism. It was offered for production to one company after another and firmly rejected. The grounds of its rejection were that it was a costume play and costume plays were not wanted and that its treatment was above the heads of the public. Indeed, every one thought at the time that Mr. Korda was mad. Since then (1933) every important producer has been making similar costume plays and films which are, apparently, above the heads of the public. Thus the sheep-like progress of the movies goes on.

The Private Life of Henry VIII was made for £59,000. Some of its scenes cost only £10 or £12. It had no highly paid stars with the exception of Charles Laughton; all the other members of the cast worked for negligible salaries and for the pleasure of the adventure.

The picture, as every one knows, has affected talkies profoundly, and enjoyed an astonishing success all over the world. It proved that an intelligent film, finely photographed and well produced, could appeal to vast multitudes of film-goers despite the fact that their tastes had been ruined by countless reels of sickly celluloid. It proved that a film could be made for very little money if brains, artistry, and enthusiasm were behind it. (The average machine-made American movie—what is known as the 'programme picture'—costs about the same price, between £40,000 and £60,000, but is no longer voted a big 'money-maker'.)

In *The Private Life of Henry VIII* we have a film of taste, of wit, of good, boisterous humour, as English as a Sussex field. Technically it is first rate, without attempting anything unusual in photography or cutting, or deafening the ear with the obtrusive technique of the Russian school.

What does it suggest above all? What new thing does it bring into pictures? It suggests a film made by men of culture, for the love and excitement of making it, but culture without decadence or any retreat from the vulgarity of the period. More important still, it sowed the seeds of

a tradition—a tradition as remote from the bought scholar-
ship of Hollywood as Shakespeare is from Ella Wheeler
Wilcox.

The cinema badly needs such a tradition, for it is repeat-
ing itself out of its own nothingness. Only the opportunity
to study its workings at leisure can keep that ideal alive
and give sense to the whole hilarious exercise of film-
making. We should be able to pin down and observe the
movement of a film long after it has fluttered past the eye
and intrigued the ear. The amateur film producer, of
whom there are many thousands in this country and
abroad, the man or woman who goes every week to the
pictures, should be able, as it were, to hold a film in his
hands as well as in his memory and live over again its best
moments. The film passes by; it dies as it goes and leaves
not a wrack behind. Here, at all events, is one that has
made film history—and there are more to come. There is
H. G. Wells's *Whither Mankind?* and Bernard Shaw's film
of *St. Joan.* These, to which *Henry VIII* was a prelude and
a spur, announce the beginnings of a new screen literature.
Whereas yesterday it was the fashion to see and hear a
film; to-day there is no reason why, if the film is good, we
should not read it as well.

ERNEST BETTS

ILLUSTRATIONS

GLOSSARY

The following terms and abbreviations, out of many in common use, are introduced in this script:

SHOT, SHOOTING: Photograph; photographing the picture.

CLOSE SHOT, CLOSE-UP: Object or part of an object photographed so that it covers the whole of the screen.

MEDIUM SHOT: Scene in middle distance; photographing the character so that about half or two-thirds of the figure is shown.

LONG SHOT: Shooting from a distance.

FULL SHOT: Complete group of people or crowded scene filling the screen.

TRACKING or TRUCKING SHOT: Movement of the camera forwards or backwards to follow any object in motion.

PAN or PANNING: Swinging the camera horizontally or vertically.

DETAIL SHOT: Photograph of some detail, a clock, a telephone, a signature, etc., to emphasize any point in the action.

EXT.: Exterior.

INT.: Interior.

DISSOLVE: One scene slowly fading into another.

FADE-IN and FADE-OUT: Scene becoming visible from a blank screen or disappearing from a full screen.

FLASHES: Rapid details giving a glimpse of the scene from different angles; quick impressionistic shots.

THE CAST

HENRY VIII	CHARLES LAUGHTON
THOMAS CULPEPER . . .	ROBERT DONAT
THOMAS CROMWELL . . .	FRANKLIN DYALL
WRIOTHESLY	MILES MANDER
ARCHBISHOP CRANMER . . .	LAWRENCE HANRAY
DUKE OF CLEVES . . .	WILLIAM AUSTIN
PEYNELL	JOHN LODER
CORNELL	CLAUDE ALLISTER
FRENCH EXECUTIONER . .	GIBB McLAUGHLIN
ENGLISH EXECUTIONER . . .	SAM LIVESEY
KINGSTON	WILLIAM HEUGHAN
ANNE BOLEYN	MERLE OBERON
The Second Wife	
JANE SEYMOUR	WENDY BARRIE
The Third Wife	
ANNE OF CLEVES . . .	ELSA LANCHESTER
The Fourth Wife	
KATHERINE HOWARD . . .	BINNIE BARNES
The Fifth Wife	
KATHERINE PARR . . .	EVERLEY GREGG
The Sixth Wife	
THE NURSE	LADY TREE

Presented for the first time in London
at the
LEICESTER SQUARE THEATRE
OCTOBER 24, 1933

THE PRIVATE LIFE OF
HENRY VIII

Dissolve to

TITLE 1

Henry VIII had six wives. Catherine of Aragon was the first; but her story is of no particular interest— she was a respectable woman. So Henry divorced her.

He then married Anne Boleyn. This marriage also was a failure, but not for the same reason.

Fade-in

INT. ROYAL BEDCHAMBER— MORNING

SCENE 1—MEDIUM SHOT

Camera shooting towards the bed-hangings, with embroidered corners 'H' and 'A' above the bed. Trucking back till the camera shows the bed.

SCENE 2—MEDIUM SHOT

Camera shooting towards the door of the bedchamber. The door opens and the Old Nurse peeps cautiously into the room. She makes sure that nobody is in the room. She enters and beckons to unseen people outside the door. Half-a-dozen ladies-in-waiting enter. They look round the room with great interest.

SCENE 3—FULL SHOT

The young ladies approach the bed, the Old Nurse leading them. It is a very exciting adventure for the young ladies. When they get near to the bed, the Old Nurse turns her head and indicates the bed, as if to say: Here it is!

SCENE 4—MEDIUM SHOT

Old Nurse with a very spirited young lady. She follows the Old Nurse into the immediate proximity of the bed. The Old Nurse smiles at her encouragingly. She is all excitement, but speaks at last:

1ST LADY: So that's the King's bed.

NURSE: Yes, my dear. (*Slips her hand down the bed.*) And he has not long left it—feel!

The girl feels the warm sheets. Her eyes are creating a picture—there is a tiny pause before she speaks. Other girls now come into the picture, feeling more at ease.

1ST LADY: I wonder what he looks like—in bed.

2ND LADY (*a rival beauty*): *You'll* never know!

1ST LADY (*annoyed*): Well, there's no need to be spiteful, is there, Mistress Nurse?

NURSE (*consolingly*): No, my dear; and you've as good a chance as another when

the King's in one of his
merry moods.

The girls laugh.

1ST LADY (*covered with real or mock confusion*): *Oh!* I never meant
—I never thought——

2ND LADY: *Didn't* you, darling?

*The second lady looks as though
she were going to slap the other
girl's face, but the Old Nurse
bustles between them to the bed and
catches hold of the coverlet.*

NURSE: Now, Ladies! You're not
here to quarrel, but to get
busy with your needles.
(*Business.*) Look—all these
'A's' must come out, and
'J's' go in. Hurry, Ladies,
hurry!

SCENE 5—FULL SHOT
*The young ladies go to work now
with all their instincts unfettered.
They are gathering up the linen,
taking down the hangings. Suppressed laughter accompanies their
whispers.*

SCENE 6—MEDIUM SHOT
*Two young ladies who have not
spoken yet, holding the embroidered
'H' and 'A' in their hands.*

SCENE 7—DETAIL SHOT
*The embroidered 'H' and 'A' in
the young ladies' hands.*

SCENE 8—MEDIUM SHOT
Back to the young ladies who examine the two letters closely.

> 3RD LADY: Anne Boleyn dies this morning.   Jane Seymour takes her place to-night! What luck!
>
> 4TH LADY: For which of them?

EXT. TOWER—MORNING

SCENE 9—LONG SHOT
The Tower from a special angle, looming up massive and menacing.

EXT. TOWER GREEN—
    MORNING

SCENE 10—FULL SHOT
Tower Green with the scaffold and the block.   Guests begin to arrive. Officers of the Tower place them according to their ranks.

INT. ANNE BOLEYN'S ROOM IN
    THE TOWER—MORNING

SCENE 11—MEDIUM SHOT
Anne Boleyn with her four ladies. She is sitting in front of her mirror, the ladies busy with her hair.

SCENE 12—CLOSE SHOT
Anne looking into the mirror, and trying to get a back-view of her head.

ANNE: The hand-mirror——

She stretches out her hand for the mirror to Lady Marbury, who gives it to her. Anne examines the back-view of her head.

Will the net be strong enough to keep my hair in place when—when my head falls?

LADY MARBURY: Y—yes, Madam. (*Struggles with her tears.*)

ANNE (*looking first at her full face and then her profile in the mirror*): I do hope it will. (*She catches the sound of a sob from one of the ladies.*) Don't! . . . (*She herself is having a terrible struggle to preserve her composure.*) Please!

SCENE 13—MEDIUM SHOT
Anne rises. The ladies fighting their tears.

LADY MARBURY: You're so brave, Madam.

ANNE: Well, would you have me lose my head, just because I'm to—lose my head?

She makes a pitiful little attempt to smile. Her ladies are in tears.

INT. ARMOURY IN THE TOWER
    —MORNING

SCENE 14—FULL SHOT
The French executioner is laying his blade on the grindstone, which

is being turned by his English assistant. He withdraws the blade, makes it whip and whistle through the air, runs his thumb along the edge and shows it with pride to his very sulky English assistant, who, throughout the scene, regards him with resentment and contempt. They should be contrasting types— the Frenchman very supple and willowy, the Englishman very square and powerful.

SCENE 15—MEDIUM SHOT
The English assistant sulky and silent. The French executioner speaks at last.

EXECUTIONER (*with pride*): There's a blade for you! Fit for a King—or—in this case— a Queen! Is it not?

ASSISTANT: Not fit for *our* Queen.

EXECUTIONER (*surprised*): No? Why not?

ASSISTANT: She's an English Queen, isn't she? Well, what's wrong with English steel? And, come to that, what's wrong with an English headsman?

EXECUTIONER: Meaning yourself?

ASSISTANT: Why not? I was good enough to knock off the Queen's five lovers, wasn't I? Then why do they want you over—a Frenchman from Calais!

He spits on the grindstone with
savage contempt.

EXECUTIONER: I will tell you——

ASSISTANT *(interrupting him and tapping*
him on the chest): *I'm* telling
you! It's a damned shame,
with half the English
executioners out of work
as it is!

EXECUTIONER *(very angrily)*: And *why* are
they out of work? Because
they are only fit to sever the
bull-necks of their country-
men with a butcher's
cleaver! But a *woman's*
neck, a *Queen's* neck—that
calls for *finesse*, for delicacy,
for *chivalry*—(*He kisses his*
fingertips)—in one word—a
Frenchman!

ASSISTANT: I can think of *another* word!

EXT. TOWER GREEN—
MORNING

SCENE 16—FULL SHOT
More and more sightseers arriving.
The officers have a hard task to find
places for them. The scaffold and
block in the background.

SCENE 17—MEDIUM SHOT
A man and his wife. They have
been placed, as it were, in the front
row of the Pit.

WIFE (*with deep feeling*): *Poor* Anne Boleyn! I do feel so sorry for her!

She bends over the woman in front of her.

Would you mind taking off your hat, Madam—we can't see the block. . . .

SCENE 18—CLOSE SHOT

The lady addressed and the wife. The former decides, in spite of her offended dignity, to take off her hat. It is a victory for the wife.

WIFE: Thank you so much.

SCENE 19—MEDIUM SHOT

Back to the wife and the husband.

WIFE: Is it true that the King marries Jane Seymour to-morrow?

HUSBAND: To-day, they say.

WIFE: *To-day?*

HUSBAND: Yes. (*Enviously.*) What it is to be a King!

The wife looks at him with wifely resentment.

WIFE: Meaning what?

INT. GREAT HALL, HAMPTON COURT—MORNING

SCENE 20—FULL SHOT

The young ladies busy embroidering the King's bed-linen with the new initials. Among them is Katherine Howard.

SCENE 21—MEDIUM SHOT

A group of young ladies busy work-
ing and talking.

> 1ST LADY: Anne Boleyn—was she
> guilty, do you think?
>
> 2ND LADY: All her lovers confessed.
>
> KATHERINE: Under torture.   I believe
> she was as innocent as you
> or I.
>
> 2ND LADY: Thank you for the compli-
> ment.
>
> 1ST LADY: You think she dies so that
> the King may be free to
> marry Lady Jane Sey-
> mour?
>
> 2ND LADY: Yes, she thinks that's what
> they mean when they say
> 'Chop and change!'
>
> KATHERINE: Don't!   It's no jesting
> matter.

INT. ARMOURY IN THE TOWER
—MORNING

SCENE 22—MEDIUM SHOT

The French executioner and his
English assistant.   The French
executioner reaches for his mask.

SCENE 23—CLOSE SHOT

The executioner whistling a little
tune as he adjusts the mask over his
eyes.

INT. CORRIDOR AT HAMPTON
  COURT—MORNING

SCENE 24—MEDIUM SHOT
We hear the same tune whistled.
Henry swaggers into the picture
from the direction of the camera.

SCENE 25—LONG SHOT
The King swaggering down the
corridor whistling.

INT. GREAT HALL, HAMPTON
  COURT—MORNING

SCENE 26—MEDIUM SHOT
The same group of ladies busy
embroidering. Katherine Howard
among them.

1ST LADY:	Jane Seymour of all people! Whatever could the King see in her?
2ND LADY:	Oh, she's very sweet.
1ST LADY:	Yes, but does the King *like* sugar with his milk and water?
3RD LADY:	Listen! Wasn't that the gun?
KATHERINE:	What gun?
3RD LADY:	When Anne Boleyn's head falls a gun is to be fired from the Tower, another at Westminster and a third at Richmond. So that the

King may know as soon as he is free to marry Jane.

KATHERINE: What a pretty arrangement! The joint goes out—Bang! The Sweets come in!

1ST LADY: Katherine!

SCENE 27—MEDIUM SHOT

Camera shooting towards the door. Henry enters unobserved. He stops and listens.

SCENE 28—MEDIUM SHOT

Back to the group of young ladies.

KATHERINE (*indignantly*): Well, if the King were not a king what would you call him?

1ST LADY: What would *you* call him?

KATHERINE: I'll tell you——

She follows the frightened look of her companions. She sees the King.

SCENE 29—LONG SHOT

Henry coming in to the room. Ladies rising and curtsying. Deathly silence. Henry reaches Katherine.

SCENE 30—MEDIUM SHOT

Henry and Katherine. Katherine has risen and curtsied with the others. She is now nearly fainting. In the background the other young ladies, very much frightened.

HENRY: No. Tell *me*.

Katherine unable to speak. She lowers her head. He signs to the ladies to rise.

(*To Katherine.*) If I were not a king, what then?——All right, Ladies. Come here!

He takes her chin between his fingers and thumb, and forces her to look him in the eyes.

Look at me. . . . What would you call me?

SCENE 31—CLOSE SHOT

Henry and Katherine. Katherine looks into his eyes and begins to gather some desperate strength. She looks straight into his eyes.

HENRY: Well, what would you call me?

KATHERINE: I should call you—Your Majesty—a *man*.

HENRY (*laughing*): Why, so I am— and glad of it!

SCENE 32—MEDIUM SHOT

He swaggers away in great good humour, then turns back to her.

HENRY: And you may be glad of it too, one day. Blushing, hey? She must be new to the Court. What is your name, wench?

KATHERINE: Katherine Howard, if it please Your Majesty.

HENRY: It does, Katherine. It does.

SCENE 33—LONG SHOT
Henry goes out. The girls rush and crowd round Katherine with congratulations, etc.

EXT.   NEAR THE TOWER—MORNING

SCENE 35—MEDIUM SHOT
Guards with drummers.

SCENE 36—DETAIL SHOT
Drummers drumming.

EXT. TOWER GREEN—MORNING

SCENE 37—MEDIUM SHOT
The scaffold, and a few men busy with the last arrangements.

SCENE 38—DETAIL SHOT
The men's hands tapping nails into the scaffold in the same rhythm as the drumming.

EXT.   WINDOW OF PRESENCE CHAMBER—MORNING

SCENE 39—CLOSE SHOT
The King's hands drumming with his fingers on the window-panes in the same rhythm.

SCENE 40—MEDIUM SHOT
Camera shooting through the window and showing that the hands belong to Henry.

INT. PRESENCE CHAMBER

SCENE 41—MEDIUM SHOT
Henry at the window. He turns. Camera pans and shows Cromwell, Cranmer and other ministers in a group. Henry enters the picture.

HENRY: No, Cromwell. If England were as rich as Portugal or as big as Spain, then we could afford such luxuries. But England is too small a country—three million souls in all—for us to impose our will on Europe.

CROMWELL: Yet you want Dover fortified, sir.

HENRY: I do.

CROMWELL: And the Fleet doubled.

HENRY: Ay. Ships and ships and then *more* ships.

CROMWELL: But the cost!

HENRY (*with contempt*): You and your costs! Listen, man— the French and Germans are at each other's throats again. They may hate each other for another twenty years.

CROMWELL: There lies our safety.

> HENRY: For the moment.   But one
> day they may forget their
> hatred of each other in
> their hatred of us.   To
> guard against that day will
> cost us money.   To leave
> ourselves unguarded will
> cost us England.

SCENE 42—LONG SHOT
*Henry walks back and forth
thoughtfully.*

SCENE 43—DETAIL SHOT
A clock chiming.

SCENE 44—MEDIUM SHOT
*Henry stops in mid-stride, arrested
by the sound, then swings round.*

> HENRY: Thomas Culpeper!

Culpeper steps forward.

> See what has become of
> the Queen.

> CULPEPER (*surprised*):   There — there
> will be a gunshot, Your
> Majesty.

> HENRY (*angrily*): Fool!   I didn't
> mean—I meant, see if the
> Lady Jane is ready.

Culpeper bows and goes.

INT. THE QUEEN'S ROOM AT
HAMPTON COURT—MORNING

SCENE 45—MEDIUM SHOT

Jane Seymour, the Old Nurse, and ladies-in-waiting. The last touches being put to the wedding-dress.

A LADY: And now your head-dress, Madam——

JANE: Yes. Now which shall it be —the pearl chaplet or the velvet coif?

LADY: Oh, the *chaplet*!

2ND LADY: Oh, the *coif*!

The ladies look towards the door. Camera pans to the door. Culpeper enters.

CULPEPER: The King wishes to know whether you are ready, Madam.

Jane comes into the picture.

JANE: But I don't know whether to wear the pearls or the—— Of course! I'll ask the King!

She snatches up both head-dresses and runs out, followed by Culpeper.

INT. PRESENCE CHAMBER— MORNING

SCENE 46—MEDIUM SHOT
Henry, his Ministers and Bishops.

HENRY: A strong fort at Dover, a strong Fleet in the Channel, and we can laugh in their

faces.   But the money—
the money—we *must* have
the money!

CROMWELL: New taxes, sir?

HENRY: New taxes?   My people are
bled white already!   Yet a
way must be found—*must*
be found. . . .

*There is a worried silence while
he paces the room.   Struck by a
thought he turns quickly to his
Ministers.*

Listen!   There *is* one way
—I shrink from using it,
My Lord of Norfolk—but
needs must when—— (*The
door flies open, and he cries*)
The Devil!

SCENE 47—MEDIUM SHOT
*Camera shooting towards the door.
Jane runs gaily in, holding out a
head-dress in each hand.*

JANE: Look, Henry—*which* shall
I wear?

HENRY (*mastering a natural impulse
to throw her out of the window*):   Softly, sweetheart.
We have affairs of state
here——

JANE: What? on your wedding
morning! Oh, you *naughty*
men!   Listen, darling, this
is *really* important—shall
it be the chaplet or the
coif?   And you haven't

said a word about my dress—don't you love it? (*She fingers the front of the bodice.*)   Twenty-one little buttons—one for every year of my age! And do you like the back?   (*She turns round for inspection— Henry silently appeals to Heaven to witness that she is more than he deserves.*)

HENRY (*dryly*): Marvellous!

He turns to the Bishop, and the Camera pans to the Bishop.

HENRY: My Lord Bishop, will you await us in the chapel?

The Bishops and Ministers bow themselves out. The Camera pans back to Henry and Jane.

JANE: What a serious face! Something is troubling you! What is it?

HENRY: Nothing.   Only the need of money.

JANE (*laughing*): I *knew* you were teasing me! *Kings* have no need to think of money.

HENRY (*dryly*): No?

JANE: You know very well they don't. There are the State coffers and a King takes what he needs. Now do be serious for a moment—do you know that you haven't kissed me yet?

HENRY: That is soon remedied.

*He catches her up, holds her close,
and kisses her.*

JANE (*breathlessly*): Oh! Have a
care of my dress! (*Smooths
out her ruffles.*)   And that
reminds me.   (*Holds out
her head-dresses.*)   Which of
these?

HENRY: Why, pearls for a pearl!
Off with you, my sweet,
and put them on.   The
Bishop waits.

JANE (*at the door*): Sweetheart!
I fly!

*She runs out. The King looks
after her. He slowly turns.*

SCENE 48—MEDIUM SHOT
*Culpeper waiting in the back-
ground. Henry slowly approaches.*

HENRY: Well, Thomas?   What of
the new Queen?

CULPEPER: A marvellous woman, sir.

HENRY: Marvellous, yes.   Do you
find her beautiful?

CULPEPER: *Lovely!*

HENRY: Clever, too?

CULPEPER: A miracle of good sense,
Your Majesty.

HENRY: Liar!

He playfully pushes his palm over Culpeper's face. The latter is covered with confusion by Henry's laughter.

HENRY: No, no, Thomas! *Not* clever—thanks be to Heaven! My first Queen was dignified and drove me to the bottle. My second was ambitious, and sent me to the devil. My third is a lovable fool—I shall have peace at last, and a son to follow me if God is good!

INT. ANNE BOLEYN'S ROOM IN THE TOWER—MORNING

SCENE 49—FULL SHOT
Anne with her four ladies. They turn towards the door in breathless suspense. Kingston, Constable of the Tower, enters. He stands by the door, motionless, silent, and very grave. The four ladies shrink back in terror. Anne goes slowly towards Kingston.

SCENE 50—CLOSE SHOT
Anne and Kingston. Anne talks with great exertion.

ANNE: Is it—time?

Kingston nods.

ANNE: The Headsman—they tell me he is very skilful.

MERLE OBERON AS ANNE BOLEYN

KINGSTON: Very. (*With deep compassion.*) You will suffer no pain, Madam. It is over in a breath.

ANNE (*with a pitiful little smile*): And I have such a little neck, haven't I?

EXT. TOWER GREEN—
MORNING

SCENE 51—MEDIUM SHOT

The groups near the door. They stop chattering and turn towards the door.

SCENE 52—LONG SHOT

All eyes turned in suspense towards the door through which the cortège arrives. First the Queen's Almoner, then Kingston with Anne, followed by her four ladies.

SCENE 53—MEDIUM SHOT

Anne and Kingston—Anne coming from the interior gloom into the glaring sunlight is momentarily dazed. She puts her hand over her eyes and then looks up into the sky. Kingston stands ready to catch her if she falls, but she makes a tremendous effort and walks firmly forward.

ANNE: What a lovely day!

They proceed on their way.

INT. GREAT HALL—MORNING

SCENE 54—LONG SHOT

Jane Seymour enters in the full pomp of a young bride. Her ladies follow her. The ladies in the room ready to join the cortège and go into the chapel. For the time being they curtsy to the approaching Jane.

SCENE 55—MEDIUM SHOT

Ladies in the room curtsying to Jane. Jane, still unaccustomed to being a Queen, wants to say something amiable.

JANE: Lovely day, isn't it?

LADIES: Lovely indeed, Madam.

The sound of the gun is heard. Everybody deeply impressed. The elderly ladies behind Jane cross themselves. The younger ones, including Jane, do the same.

SCENE 56—MEDIUM SHOT

Camera shooting towards the door. Between guards at attention a gentleman usher appears.

GENT. USHER (*announcing*): His Majesty, the King.

Behind him Henry enters, followed by Culpeper and three other Gentlemen of the Privy Chamber.

SCENE 57—LONG SHOT

Henry among the deeply bowing ladies goes to Jane. He takes her hand. They go and their cortège follows them.

INT. ROYAL BEDCHAMBER— NIGHT

SCENE 58—MEDIUM SHOT

Camera taking in the bed and trucking up to the hanging over the bed. We see in a Close Shot the new initials embroidered on the hangings, an 'H' and a 'J'.

SCENE 59—FULL SHOT

Under the supervision of Cornell, the Master of the Bedchamber, the royal bed is being prepared for the night. Servant girls (not ladies-in-waiting) do the work, guided and urged by an elderly woman, Mrs. Barton. They place the pillows, and spread the coverlet. A yeoman with a torch, another with candles.

SCENE 60—MEDIUM SHOT

The servant girls do the work in a gay mood, whispering and giggling. Mr. Cornell very dignified. He obviously disapproves of the servant-girls' wantonness, but it is beneath his dignity to interfere. Mrs. Barton looks at him, however, with some apprehension. She urges the girls to finish their business. She now turns towards Mr. Cornell in the attitude of a soldier reporting to an officer. The servant-girls troop out of the picture.

CORNELL: Is all in readiness?

MRS. BARTON: All but the warming and scenting of the sheets.

CORNELL: Let it be done.

Mrs. Barton turns towards the door.

SCENE 61—MEDIUM SHOT
Mrs. Barton near the bed, turning towards the door.

MRS. BARTON: The rose-water.

Two girls enter the picture with bowls of rose-water. They go to the bed.

Turn back the sheets.

The two girls sprinkle rose-water on the sheets and pillows.

The charcoal.

Two other girls come forward with warming pans. The first two girls withdraw, and the two in the picture pass the warming pans backwards and forwards over the sheets. Mrs. Barton dismisses them and turns again to Cornell.

SCENE 62—MEDIUM SHOT
Mrs. Barton reporting again to Cornell.

MRS. BARTON: Ready, Mr. Cornell.

CORNELL (*grand and gracious*): Thank you, Mrs. Barton.

Mrs. Barton goes with the feeling of a well-fulfilled duty. Cornell in solitary grandeur casts an attentive look at the bed and turns towards the ante-room.

CORNELL (*calling*): Officer!

An officer of the guards enters the picture. Cornell gravely invites him to do his duty. The officer approaches the royal bed with a rapier in his hand. He passes his rapier under the bed, behind it, and everywhere where a hidden murderer might be lurking. He finishes his work, and turns to Cornell, indicating that he has found no living soul under or behind the bed. Cornell nods his thanks, and the officer salutes him with his rapier and withdraws.

SCENE 63—FULL SHOT

The officer withdrawing. Cornell with great dignity approaches the bed and makes a last examination, perfect expert that he is. He sniffs the perfume, and puts his hand into the bed to see whether it is warm.

SCENE 64—MEDIUM SHOT

The door through which the officer went out is opened by the Old Nurse.

She enters and goes, full of confidence, towards the bed. Camera panning with her takes in Cornell, who has finished his inspection and is ready to leave. He is startled by the presence of the Old Nurse. He almost loses his dignity.

CORNELL: Here! What's this? None may come near the King's marriage-bed once it is made ready.

NURSE: But it is *not* made ready.

CORNELL: *What?* Then what do you suppose *I* have been doing for the last hour?

NURSE: Swallowing the poker by the look of you!

CORNELL (*furious*): Hold your shrewish tongue and begone! Come, out you go, my good woman! (*He tries to bustle her out; she resists him stoutly.*)

NURSE: Oh, no, I don't! And whom are you calling a 'good woman'. (*Indignantly*) a pretty name to give one who has been forty years with the King!

CORNELL: Pretty or not, you cannot stay here. What is it you want?

NURSE: Why, have you never heard of my famous charms?

CORNELL: No. Any charms you ever

had have long since
vanished.

NURSE: Not so long either! And I
charmed better men than
you in my time or I should
have drowned their chil-
dren!

CORNELL: Old vixen!

NURSE: But what I have here is not
a charm of face or figure,
but a charm of magic.

CORNELL (*scornfully*): Magic!

NURSE: Ay, magic—to put under
the King's pillow and make
it certain that he will get
a son.

CORNELL: Pooh! Such things come
about by *chance*.

NURSE: *Some* sons come by chance,
Master Cornell, as we
know—(*He makes a furious
gesture*)—Oh, I meant
nothing personal—but the
Prince of Wales must not be
left to chance. So——

*She goes towards the bed with the
charm. Cornell lays his hand on
her arm.*

CORNELL: But how do I know that
this is your purpose——?

NURSE: Fool! Would *I* harm the
King—who nursed him
from his birth?

CORNELL: Leave your accursed charm then, and begone!

The Nurse slips her charm under the pillow and turns to Cornell with a triumphant smile.

Out with you. At any moment the Queen's ladies may bring her in.

SCENE 65—OUT

INT. ROOM AT HAMPTON COURT —DAY

SCENE 66—MEDIUM SHOT
The royal bed dissolves into a child's cot or cradle. In the cradle a new-born baby. Smiling faces round the cradle, looking down at the baby; some elderly ladies, the King's doctor, Cromwell, Wriothesly.

CROMWELL: Send for the King.

Dissolve to
EXT. A GLADE IN A FOREST— DAY

SCENE 67—LONG SHOT
Henry and a small cavalcade out hawking.

SCENE 68—CLOSE SHOT
Henry on horseback looks skyward, shading his eyes with his hand.

Scene 69—Very Long Shot
*The hawk swooping down on some
quarry.*

Scene 70—Medium Shot
*Henry on horseback, looking sky-
ward. In the background his retinue
follow his look.*

Henry *(enthusiastically)*: Good bird!
She has him! She has him
for a ducat!

Scene 71—Medium Shot
*A horseman in the royal livery
arriving at a hill near the glade.
He looks for the King's party. He
hears the King's voice, and turns
towards the party.*

Scene 72—Long Shot
*The horseman in the royal livery
galloping towards the King's party.*

Scene 73—Long Shot
*Henry and his party, still engrossed
in the sight of the hawk's flight.
They look skyward. One or two
gentlemen perceive the approaching
horseman and hesitate whether to tell
the King. Henry notices the horseman only when he gallops into the
picture. His first reaction is one of
slight irritation. He does not like
surprises.*

SCENE 74—MEDIUM SHOT
The horseman, however, pulls the horse up on to its haunches, leaps down, and kneels, cap in hand.

HORSEMAN (*panting, but enthusiastic*): A boy, Your Majesty.

SCENE 75—MEDIUM SHOT
Henry looking down at the man. He utters a shout of joy.

HENRY: A boy! By God, a boy!

He wrenches his horse round and strikes in the spurs, then checks it for a moment to throw the messenger his purse.

SCENE 76—LONG SHOT
Henry throwing his purse to the messenger. He dashes off at full gallop. His retinue are for the moment lost in amazement, then they gallop after him. They gallop out of the picture.

SCENE 77
The messenger gathering up the coins which were spilt all over the grass when the purse fell.

EXT.   VILLAGE STREET—DAY

SCENE 78—LONG SHOT
Village people stopped by the sight of the approaching cavalcade. They

*look towards the horsemen with
attention. They state that it is the
King.*

SCENE 79—LONG SHOT
*Henry leading his cavalcade. They
ride at full gallop through the
village.*

HENRY (*shouting*): A boy, men!

*They thunder through the picture.
The village people amazed. A
gentleman of the King's retinue
shouts a few words completing the
information!*

GENTLEMAN: *The Prince of Wales!*

He gallops out of the picture.

SCENE 80—LONG SHOT
*The cavalcade disappearing. An
outburst of enthusiasm among the
village people.*

VOICES: A boy! The Prince of
Wales! Long live the King!

*The shouts grow to a roaring outcry
of enthusiasm.*

EXT. IN FRONT OF A MANOR
   HOUSE—DAY

SCENE 81—LONG SHOT
*Ladies and gentlemen pouring out
to the road. Behind them a crowd
of tenants and servants. They apparently know already something of*

the great news. They await the approaching cavalcade with loyal enthusiasm.

VOICES: There he comes, the King! Long live the King!

Henry's cavalcade approaching.

SCENE 82—LONG SHOT

Camera shooting towards the approaching cavalcade, so that we have the impression that Henry is riding right into the camera. He is greeted by an outcry of enthusiasm which doubles his joy. He waves his hand to the waiting crowd.

HENRY (*shouting*): A boy! A boy!

He waves his hand and disappears out of the picture.

SCENE 83—LONG SHOT

The cavalcade thunders through the crowd. A terrific outburst of enthusiasm:

SHOUTS: Long live the King! Long live the Prince of Wales!

The sound of this outburst goes over into the clattering of hoofs in the next shot, growing and growing.

EXT.   BRIDGE   AT   HAMPTON COURT—NIGHT

SCENE 84—LONG SHOT

The royal cavalcade thundering over the bridge. This is the climax of

*the sound effect. After this com-
plete stillness.*

INT. CORRIDOR AT HAMPTON
    COURT—NIGHT

SCENE 85—LONG SHOT
*Camera shooting towards the en-
trance. Henry hurries in. We must
have the impression that he has
just jumped down from his horse.
He is talking as he enters.*

HENRY: Where is my boy?

*He hurries towards the camera, but
he is silent now. His pace slows
down and he looks startled. Complete silence.*

SCENE 86—MEDIUM SHOT
*In front of a door at the end of
a corridor. By the door stand the
elderly ladies who were seen round
the baby's cot, the doctor, and pos-
sibly Cromwell. They stand as
though to bar the entrance through
the door. Henry comes into the
picture.*

SCENE 87—CLOSE SHOT
*Henry and Cromwell, with the doc-
tor. Nobody dares to talk. Henry
scans their faces with misgivings
and painful hesitation.*

HENRY: My son!

Nobody moves.

3

(*Hesitating*) Is he—dead?

Cromwell looks at the doctor as if commanding him to give an answer.

DOCTOR: The Prince lives, Your Majesty, but the Queen has died.

Henry deeply moved. He tries to find words. He cannot. He turns and goes. The others look after him.

SCENE 88—LONG SHOT
Camera shooting from the viewpoint of Cromwell and the others near the door. Henry goes back down the corridor up which he has just hurried so joyfully. He walks now with stooped shoulders and lowered head.

Dissolve to
INT. ROOM AT HAMPTON COURT—DAY

SCENE 89—MEDIUM SHOT
The baby's cot. Henry enters the picture and looks down at his son.

SCENE 90—CLOSE SHOT
The smiling baby.

SCENE 91—CLOSE SHOT
Henry looking down on the child,

thoughtful, with a wry smile but
with a deep tenderness.

> HENRY: My son! . . . One day you
> will rule England—a
> greater England than mine
> —if you are strong enough
> to hold the sceptre firmly.
> See—here it is!

SCENE 92—DETAIL SHOT
Henry's hand. He gives the child
his finger, and the baby's tiny
fingers close upon it.

SCENE 93—MEDIUM SHOT
Henry and the child. Henry
laughs with delight.

> HENRY: Bravely done, my little
> Prince! That's the way of
> it. That's the grip! You
> smile, do you? Smile while
> you may, then, for you'll
> find the Throne of England
> no smiling matter!

He bends down and very gently and
compassionately kisses the child.

EXT. RIVERSIDE—DAY

SCENE 94—LONG SHOT
A beautiful portion of the riverside
at Hampton Court. Culpeper and
Katherine—Katherine sitting on a
fallen tree; Culpeper lying on the
grass.

SCENE 95

Culpeper looks up at Katherine, Katherine looks, in deep thought, to the river.

KATHERINE: Do you think he will marry again?

CULPEPER: Who?

KATHERINE: The King.

CULPEPER: Let us hope not! Three failures should convince him that he has no gift for the business.

KATHERINE: No, it was the wives who were lacking. The *right* woman could make him happy yet.

CULPEPER (*laughing*): Every woman thinks herself the right wife for every other woman's husband.

KATHERINE: He might choose a Lady of the Court.

CULPEPER (*sits upright*): He has chosen many—for a day—or at most a week. Lady Bassett is the miracle—she has lasted ten whole days, and he is still not wearied.

KATHERINE: Then it may be that he will marry her.

CULPEPER (*laughing*): What! My lady Bassett. (*He lies back on the grass and shouts with laughter.*) My good Kate! Lady Bassett!

EXT. GARDEN—DAY

SCENE 96—LONG SHOT
Young ladies by themselves and in little groups in an avenue in the garden at Hampton Court. They pretend to care only for sunshine and flowers. As a matter of fact they expect the King to come into the garden.—A little flurry; they all look towards the Palace.

SCENE 97—MEDIUM SHOT
Henry comes with the baby in his arms. He moves towards the first group of young ladies. The young ladies surround Henry and admire the baby.

SCENE 98—CLOSE SHOT
The baby. During this shot we hear the outburst of adoration from the young ladies.

LADIES (*off*): Baby. . . . Look! Is he not wonderful. He smiles, etc., etc.

This outburst is accompanied by the ridiculous sounds by which grown-up people try to induce a baby to smile.

SCENE 99—MEDIUM SHOT
Henry with the baby in his arms. The enthusiastic young ladies crowd round him.

1ST LADY (*admiring the baby with her eyes on the King*): Look! Is he not a love? His father's image!

2ND LADY: Yes, the same eyes—like windows in Heaven!

1ST LADY: Has Heaven black windows? I did not know.

3RD LADY: His father's hands, too! And his deep chest! And see, the same legs! And the same . . .

HENRY: Madam! Not before the child!

General laughter in which Henry takes part. At the same time he proceeds on his walk with the baby.

SCENES 100 and 101—OUT

SCENE 102—LONG SHOT
Camera shooting towards the Palace. The Old Nurse hurries towards Henry and his ladies.

SCENE 103—MEDIUM SHOT
The Old Nurse hurries into the picture. Henry cowed. The Old Nurse descends upon them and snatches the child from the King's arms without ceremony.

NURSE (*indignantly*): A pretty thing—to hold the child hatless in the blazing sun!

(*To the baby*) There, lovey!
Come to one who loves
you!

*She cuddles the child and shades
his head: Then attacks the King:*

Have you lost your wits to
treat him so?

HENRY (*like a naughty child*): Why,
I never thought——

NURSE: You never *thought*! What
are brains for but to think
with? But no—you must
strut among your light o'
loves, while my poor babe
roasts in your arms.

HENRY: *Your* poor babe! *My son!*

NURSE (*with scathing contempt*): *Your
son! My CHARM!!*

EXT. RIVERSIDE—DAY

SCENE 104—MEDIUM SHOT
*Katherine and Culpeper at the
riverside. Katherine still sitting
on the fallen tree. Culpeper at her
feet.*

CULPEPER (*fondly*): Sweet Katherine!
Do you know how beauti-
ful you are?

KATHERINE (*laughing*): Oh, keep your
flatteries for the Court
ladies.

CULPEPER: Is there one beauty at the
Court with eyes like wet
violets? With hands so soft

and slender? (*He seizes her hands.*) With so sweet a shape, so fair a bosom?

He is gradually increasing his attack, and now almost has her in his arms.

With a mouth to drive a man mad?

Katherine rises. Culpeper is on his feet too. He crushes her to him, and tries to possess her mouth. She pushes him away.

KATHERINE: Tom! I think you are mad! I have given you no right to—to——

CULPEPER: Oh, but you will! (*Pleading*) Some day you will love me a little who love you so much!

KATHERINE: Some day—who knows what life may bring me? A crown perhaps.

CULPEPER: Do you mean that?

KATHERINE: Well, stranger things have happened.

CULPEPER: In dreams.

KATHERINE: In dreams that have come true.

CULPEPER: And if you got your crown, what would it be worth without love?

KATHERINE: Love is not all the world, Tom.

CULPEPER: It is—or it is nothing!

INT. A ROOM IN THE PALACE—
DAY

SCENE 104A—CLOSE SHOT
*Henry is being shaved by the Royal
Barber.*

BARBER: One moment, Your Grace.
You're keeping your hair
very well, Your Grace! I
just met His Highness the
Prince of Wales out with
his nurse this morning.
He'll have a nice head of
hair one day—if he lives
to enjoy it.

HENRY: Why shouldn't he?

BARBER: No reason at all, Your
Grace, no reason at all.
Let's hope he may, being
as he's the only one—at
least for the present.

HENRY: What do you mean—'for
the present'?

BARBER: Well, as I was saying at the
last meeting of the Barbers'
Guild only yesterday —
having a family's like having a shave—once you've
started there's no leaving
off in the middle. . . .

HENRY (*rising angrily*): Do you
presume to suggest that I
should marry again?

BARBER: That's what we think,
Your Grace!

HENRY: Well, *GET OUT!*

*Henry kicks the shaving pot, etc.,
out of his hand. The Barber flies
for his life.*

HENRY: *Marry again!*

EXT.   KITCHEN YARD—
  AFTERNOON

SCENE 105—LONG SHOT
*Pigs, chickens, geese, sheep driven
into kitchen yard.*

Dissolve to
INT.   KITCHEN—AFTERNOON

SCENE 106—MEDIUM SHOT
*Pigs, chicken, geese, sheep, slaugh-
tered and hanging on the walls of
the kitchen, ready to be turned into
food. Camera trucking back and
showing male and female members
of the kitchen staff at their work
already, chattering and laughing.*

SCENE 107—MEDIUM SHOT
*Camera shooting towards the en-
trance. A page comes in. Cooks
near the entrance turn towards him
directly he begins to speak.*

PAGE: The dinner had best be
good to-night, or some of
you will suffer.

A COOK: God save us all! Is the
King in one of his black
moods?

> PAGE: Black as ink! They have been at him to marry again.

WOMAN COOK: Poor soul!

SCENE 108—CLOSE SHOT
A pastry-cook busy at his work.

> PASTRY-COOK (*admiring his own pie-crust*): Ay, marriage is like pastry —one must be born to it!

SCENE 109—CLOSE SHOT
Another cook busy with a large pot.

> 2ND COOK: More like one of these French stews, you never know what you're getting until it's too late!

SCENE 110—MEDIUM SHOT
A carver at work, his wife near him.

> CARVER: Still, I think a man should try for another son or two —if he is a King. Eh, wife?

> HIS WIFE: Yes, my man, and even if he is not a King! (*Laughter.*)

SCENE 111—MEDIUM SHOT
A third cook working and taking part in the general laughter. A kitchen-boy assisting him in his work.

> 3RD COOK. I know what will soften his temper—a fat goose, well sauced.

KITCHEN-BOY: He needs no more geese—
Norfolk and Cromwell are
with him already!

COOK (*pinches his ear*): Then he
needs no more sauce, so
you learn to curb your
tongue! Fetch me that
trencher!

SCENE 112—MEDIUM SHOT
*Camera shooting once more towards
the pigs, chickens, geese, etc.,
hanging on the wall.*

Dissolve to
INT. CORRIDOR—EVENING

SCENE 113—MEDIUM SHOT
*Train of servitors bearing dishes to
the dining-hall. On the dishes the
same animals we have seen before,
now cooked, trimmed, and ready to
be consumed. The train of servitors go past the camera.*

Dissolve to
INT. DINING-HALL—EVENING

SCENE 114—FULL SHOT
*Servitors busy with the dishes.
Guests busy eating. There is,
however, an atmosphere of gloom
and apprehension in the room.
Ladies and gentlemen are eating,
but casting from time to time a*

look towards Henry, who is seated on a dais, flanked by Cromwell and Norfolk.

SCENE 115—MEDIUM SHOT

Henry on his dais with Cromwell and Norfolk. Henry scowling, but eating voraciously. There is a pile of dishes before him. Cromwell and Norfolk silent. Henry pushes away his empty plate with a gesture of disgust. He punches a chicken in the breast.

> HENRY: Pah! What with the cooking and the company I can touch nothing!

Still grasping a bone, he turns to his house-steward, who waits behind his chair.

> HENRY (*punching a chicken in the breast*): Call this a capon? Look at that! All sauce and no substance——

He tears off a leg.

> —like one of Cromwell's speeches—and just as difficult to swallow.

He tears it limb from limb.

> Too many cooks, that's the trouble. Above stairs as well as below.

He throws a leg over his shoulder.

> Marry again—breed more sons! Coarse brutes!

He plunges his fingers inside the bird.

There's no delicacy nowadays. No consideration for others. Refinement's a thing of the past!

He throws the carcass over his shoulder.

(*Off*) Manners are *dead*! Have the cooks whipped from the kitchen!

He swings round on Cromwell.

And *you*, Master Cromwell, you may tell my loyal Guild of Barbers to mind their own business and leave me to mine! Marry, *marry, MARRY!* Am I the King or a breeding bull?

SCENE 116—FULL SHOT
Everybody in the room silent, including Cromwell and Norfolk. Everybody stops eating.

SCENE 117—MEDIUM SHOT
Back to Henry, Cromwell and Norfolk. Silence. The house-steward puts a new dish before Henry with great caution. Henry sulkily begins to eat, throwing bones over his shoulders to the great peril of pages and servitors. Suddenly he bursts out in a blaze of temper.

HENRY: God's truth! Are you all dumb? I have known funerals merrier!

One of the gentlemen ushers comes forward.

> HENRY: Have we no singers at the Court?

SCENE 118—OUT

SCENE 119—MEDIUM SHOT

Henry and his guests. Into the picture comes Katherine with a guitar. She bows to the King and sits down near the dais, as if, so to speak, at his feet.

> HENRY: What will you sing?

> KATHERINE: Whatever pleases you—if I know the song.

> HENRY: Do you know, 'What shall I do for love?'

> KATHERINE: Yes, indeed.

> HENRY: Good music, do you think?

> KATHERINE: Yes, and lovely words.

> HENRY: Did you know that both were mine?

> KATHERINE: How should I not? It is my favourite song.

> HENRY: Then let us hear it, child.

> KATHERINE (*sings*):
> 'Alas! What shall I do for love?
> For love, alack! for love what shall I do?
> Since none are kind
> I do not find unto!
> Alack!'

SCENE 120—CLOSE SHOT
Katherine singing.

> HENRY: Very good, my child.

SCENE 121—MEDIUM SHOT
Katherine at once retires, although Henry makes a gesture as if he would like to speak to her. Culpeper behind Henry, at once delighted with Katherine and jealous of her.

SCENE 122—CLOSE SHOT
Henry turns to Culpeper.

> HENRY: What's her name, Thomas?
> CULPEPER: Katherine Howard, Your Majesty.
> HENRY: Ah, I remember——

He turns back to his guests.

SCENE 123—MEDIUM SHOT
Katherine arrives back at her place. Everybody congratulates her in hushed voices.

> VOICES: Very good, Kate — His Majesty liked it, etc.

SCENE 124—MEDIUM SHOT
Henry and his guests. Henry has finished eating. He is drinking now and contented.

> HENRY: And so, Master Cromwell, you would have me make a fourth marriage?

CROMWELL: If Your Majesty would but consider it.

HENRY: I *would* consider it — I would consider it the victory of optimism over experience.

General laughter, led by Henry.

SCENE 125—FLASHES
Everybody laughing in the room and outside the room, down to the kitchen.

SCENE 126—MEDIUM SHOT
Back to Henry, Cromwell and Norfolk.

CROMWELL: But we need more heirs . . .

HENRY: I have given you three—two daughters and a son. I grant you the daughters show little promise. Mary may grow to wisdom, but Elizabeth will never learn to rule so much as a kitchen! But the boy, he is my second self.

CROMWELL: True, sir, but a third self, and maybe a fourth, would make all safe.

HENRY: What is your project then?

He smiles and everybody at the table smiles.

4

SCENE 127—CLOSE SHOT

Henry, Cromwell and Norfolk.
The conversation about the marriage
prospects flows more easily.

> CROMWELL: The Duchess of Cleves.

> HENRY (*pondering*): Have you a portrait of her?

> CROMWELL: No.

> HENRY: Send Holbein to paint her. And Peynell to watch Holbein.

> CROMWELL: Your Grace has no faith in German painters?

> HENRY: Yes, but I have no faith in German beauty.

He laughs. Everybody laughs with him.

> HENRY (*calling*): Peynell!

SCENE 128—MEDIUM SHOT

Henry, Cromwell and Norfolk.
Peynell hurries into picture.

> PEYNELL: Your Majesty.

> HENRY: I want you to go over to Cleves. I might marry the Duchess . . .

Dissolve.

EXT. GARDEN AT CLEVES—
DAY

SCENE 129—LONG SHOT

A double row of sunflowers. Peynell with Anne of Cleves. They

approach the camera.   Anne carries
a riding-whip.

ANNE (*with great spirit*): I will *not*
marry your King! I will
not, I will *not*, I will *not*!
(*With every 'not' she slashes
at the flowers which flank the
path.*)

PEYNELL: But why? There is not a
Princess in Europe would
not be eager to make such
a match.

ANNE: What! That Bluebeard!

PEYNELL (*shocked*): Princess!

ANNE (*interrupting him*): What
else is he? His first wife
divorced, his second be-
headed, his third dead in
childbirth! A pretty pros-
pect for the fourth. But
she will not be Anne of
Cleves, and so you may
tell him!

SCENE 130—MEDIUM SHOT
*Peynell with Anne. Peynell
resigned.*

PEYNELL: As you will, Princess.

ANNE: And why 'Princess'? (*Softly*)
Last night you called me
'Anne'.

PEYNELL: Last night I forgot—everything. *To-day*——

ANNE: To-day—forget everything
but last night!

INT. ROOM AT CLEVES—DAY

SCENE 131—MEDIUM SHOT

Camera shooting towards a blank canvas on an easel, and panning to Holbein and the Duke of Cleves. The Duke is obviously inclined to be furious. He stares at the blank canvas.

HOLBEIN: How can I paint Her Highness if she will not sit? When the light is good she is always in the garden with Master Peynell.

DUKE: Natürlich! He talk mit his tongue but also mit his eyes, that young man. Until he come she will not hear of this marriage, but now all goes well, I think so, isn't it?

HOLBEIN: With the marriage, maybe —but what of the portrait, Your Grace?

DUKE: Be patient. I will make it that she come already.

EXT. GARDEN AT CLEVES—DAY

SCENE 132—MEDIUM SHOT

Peynell and Anne in a close embrace. They are startled by a warning cough. They look up and break away hurriedly. Camera

pans to a lackey.   The lackey
approaches, camera panning with
him.

LACKEY (*to Anne*): May it please
Your Grace, the Duke de-
sires your presence forth-
with.

Anne answers with a nod. She goes,
followed by Peynell.

SCENE 133—LONG SHOT
Anne hurrying towards the castle.
Peynell follows her at the same
pace.   Last comes the lackey, very
leisurely.

INT. ROOM AT CLEVES—DAY

SCENE 134—LONG SHOT
Camera shooting towards the en-
trance.   The Duke is waiting here
for Anne.   In the background Hol-
bein with his easel.   Anne enters,
followed by Peynell.

SCENE 135—MEDIUM SHOT
The Duke stops Anne.   Peynell in
the background.

DUKE: Setze!

ANNE: Ich sitze schön.

She goes towards Holbein.   The
Duke indicates to Peynell that this
is the way to treat women.   He
takes him by the arm and they go
out.

SCENE 136—MEDIUM SHOT

Anne and Holbein. Anne sits in the chair prepared for her. Holbein begins his work. Anne casts a look after her brother and states that he is gone. She at once assumes a grotesque expression. Holbein, busy for a few moments arranging his canvas and materials, looks up and is amazed at what he sees.

HOLBEIN: Your Highness! Forgive me, but if the King were to see you with *that* face, it—it would not help on the marriage!

ANNE: You think she is ugly, my face?

HOLBEIN: Only when Your Highness *makes* it so.

SCENE 137

A room at Hampton Court. Holbein's portrait of Anne is on an easel. The Court is inspecting and discussing it.

COURTIER: Holbein's masterpiece!

LADY ROCHFORD: The original still in Calais?

COURTIER: Afraid of the storm in the Channel.

SCENE 138

Henry comes into the picture. Stands before portrait.

HENRY: H'm. What do you think of her?

LADY ROCHFORD: Oh, charming, Your Grace!

COURTIER: I was just saying, Your Grace, what a face!

SCENE 139—CLOSE SHOT

HENRY: Well, little Katherine, what do *you* think of the new Queen?

KATHERINE: We are very sorry, sire, that the Lady Anne cannot cross the Channel.

HENRY: H'm—I'm sorry too. . . . I'm a lonely man. When are you going to sing for me again.

KATHERINE: Any time Your Majesty orders me.

HENRY: To-night, in my rooms?

KATHERINE: Hardly the right place for singing, Your Majesty.

HENRY: Your rooms then—eleven o'clock. Not a soul will see me.

SCENE 140—CLOSE SHOT

CULPEPER: WHAT was he saying to you?

KATHERINE: Who?

CULPEPER: The King.

KATHERINE: Nothing.

CULPEPER: Nothing! I was watching you.

KATHERINE: Oh—spying!

CULPEPER: Not at all: but when I see you making yourself cheap——

KATHERINE: When you do, come and tell me, will you? And until you do, kindly keep your nose out of my private affairs!

CULPEPER: Katherine!

He seizes her arm.

KATHERINE: Please! This velvet does crush so!

SCENE 141

Henry stealing off to Katherine's room with the greatest secrecy and unexpectedly coming upon a sentry. The sentry instantly turns out the Guard, as in duty bound.

SENTRY: The King's Guard!

The Guard turns out, to Henry's great discomfiture. He salutes, and goes on his way. Climbing a stairway, he stumbles. This awakes another sentry.

SENTRY: The King's Guard!

Much the same scene repeats itself. Henry hurries away. Rounding the corner of a corridor he runs into another sentry.

SENTRY: The King's——

Henry hurriedly puts his hand over the sentry's mouth and passes on. He comes to a door. He is about

*to knock. But first he pulls out a
little mirror, arranges his hair, etc.
Meanwhile, unseen by him, a
sentry looks round the corner and
realizes exactly what is happening.
Henry knocks.*

INT. KATHERINE'S ROOM

SCENE 142

> KATHERINE: Who's that?
>
> HENRY (*off*): Henry.
>
> KATHERINE: Henry who?
>
> HENRY: The King.
>
> KATHERINE: Oh! NOT the *man*?
>
> HENRY: Unlock the door.
>
> KATHERINE: Isn't it rather late for a maid to unlock her door to a man?
>
> HENRY: Unlock the door!
>
> KATHERINE: Is it a command?
>
> HENRY: Yes.
>
> KATHERINE: To the King, then—not the man.

*She unlocks the door and Henry
comes in. She curtsies to the
ground.*

> HENRY: Don't. I left my crown outside.
>
> KATHERINE: With my reputation.
>
> HENRY: Oh, little Katherine, no one saw me, I swear!

SCENE 143

Corridor outside Katherine's room.
A little group of the King's Guard
nodding and winking in the direc-
tion of Katherine's room and
chuckling over the situation.

INT. KATHERINE'S ROOM

SCENE 144—CLOSE SHOT

HENRY: Can't you forget the Crown,
the King and everything.
You told me once I was a
man. What would you say
if I were not the King?

KATHERINE: Get out of my room! (*off*):
That's what I would say if
you were not the King.
But since you are, I expect
the King's commands.

HENRY: To command is a poor
thing in love.

KATHERINE: In love? Who is in love?

HENRY: I am—with you!

KATHERINE (*with irony*): Love eternal
—since yesterday afternoon
until to-morrow morning!

HENRY: When I say Love, I mean
love. Couldn't you love
me, Katherine?

KATHERINE: I can't love a man with a
wife.

HENRY: I haven't got a wife.

KATHERINE: The Lady Anne of Cleves?

HENRY: That woman? She's a picture—a portrait!

KATHERINE: Oh, no, Your Majesty, she is much more.

SCENE 145—MEDIUM SHOT

Culpeper steadily drinking himself into forgetfulness. Cornell with him. Cromwell enters the picture.

CROMWELL: Where is the King? Do you know?

CULPEPER: No—nor care!

CROMWELL: You're drunk! The Duchess of Cleves has crossed the Channel and is on her way to Rochester. Find the King at once!

CORNELL (*off*): That will be impossible, my lord!

Cornell whispers in Cromwell's ear.

CROMWELL: Impossible!

CULPEPER: I'll find the King, my lord. I'll tell him!

INT. KATHERINE'S ROOM

SCENE 146

HENRY: Still afraid of me, Kate?

KATHERINE: Of you? No.

HENRY: Of whom then?

KATHERINE: Of—myself—perhaps.

A knock.

> KATHERINE: Who is that?

> CULPEPER (*off*): A message for the King!

Katherine leaves Henry's embrace and throws open the door.

> CULPEPER: Great news, Your Majesty. The Lady Anne of Cleves has crossed the Channel and is on her way to Rochester.

> HENRY: Marvellous news! (*Ruefully*) You were right, little Katherine. She seems to be much more than a portrait.

INT. A ROOM AT ROCHESTER

SCENE 147—CLOSE SHOT
Anne of Cleves and Peynell, embraced.

> ANNE: It is—what you say? a pretty kettle of fishes, to be in love with one man and to have to marry another.

> PEYNELL: I know.

> ANNE: What will happen if the King finds out?

> PEYNELL: We die. But I don't mind.

> ANNE: Oh, but I do. . . . What is to be done?

> PEYNELL: What can be done? Nothing.

ANNE: How like a man—to be dead before he is killed! There is always a way out.

PEYNELL: What way?

ANNE: I don't know—but I will find it.

SCENES 148 to 152—OUT

Dissolve to

EXT. IN FRONT OF THE HOUSE AT ROCHESTER—DAY

SCENE 153—LONG SHOT

The royal cavalcade arriving. They alight. Henry is being received by the Bishop of Rochester.

SCENE 154—MEDIUM SHOT

The Bishop wants to greet the King. Henry stops his eloquence by a friendly but decisive gesture.

HENRY: Good morning, my Lord Bishop. How is the Princess?

BISHOP: Expecting Your Majesty.

INT. ANTE-ROOM TO ANNE'S ROOM AT ROCHESTER—DAY

SCENE 155—FULL SHOT

Anne's German ladies are in the room. The door from outside is pushed open. Henry, personally and impetuously, has opened it.

He bursts into the room. The Bishop only has time to follow him. The German ladies greet Henry with deep obeisances. As they emerge, one after the other, Henry looks into their faces aghast.

HENRY: One of you is not the Princess, I presume?

LADIES: Oh, nein!

HENRY: Thank heaven for that!

INT. ANNE'S ROOM AT ROCHESTER—DAY

SCENE 156—MEDIUM SHOT

Camera shooting towards the door. Henry dashes in with great expectations, takes a step or two and stops abruptly. He stares. Camera pans to Anne. Anne, with the face she put on for Holbein and a few deft touches to her hair and dress that renders her a grotesque little figure. Camera pans with her until she meets Henry. Henry masters himself. There is a mutual repulsion between them, but she curtsies to the ground and Henry—raising her—kisses her hand.

ANNE: Oh, Heinrich!

HENRY: Welcome to England, Madam! I fear you had a bad crossing.

ANNE: Ja, der vint make mit der sea some trouble—— Oh, excuse me!

HENRY: Be pleased to accept my most humble apologies.

ANNE: Oh, but it is not your fault, the Channel chopping.

HENRY: Nevertheless, I deeply regret any inconvenience that you may have been caused.

ANNE: Oh, please! It was only that the waves go so high upstairs.

HENRY: Quite. Our Channel can be very rough, when—er—it is not smooth.

ANNE: Oh, it did!

HENRY: Permit me to express the hope that a short rest will restore you to health, Madam.

ANNE: Thank you. I hope soon I shall eat again, yes?

HENRY: By all means. You have our permission to withdraw.

ANNE: Please!

Anne curtsies as before, and, as before, Henry raises her and kisses her hand. Then he goes out.

INT. ANTE-ROOM TO ANNE'S ROOM AT ROCHESTER—DAY

SCENE 157—FULL SHOT
Henry coming from Anne's room. He mastered himself as long as he

was in Anne's presence. Now his anger is rising. He dashes through the room, frightening the German ladies to death.

INT. BISHOP'S ROOM AT
  ROCHESTER—DAY

SCENE 158—FULL SHOT

Cromwell and the Bishop. Cromwell waiting in great suspense for Henry's return. His worst expectations are surpassed when Henry enters the room like a bombshell. Henry's anger has reached its highest pitch. He is livid with rage. He runs straight to Cromwell. The Bishop retires, frightened.

Henry storms up and down, then returns with increased rage to Cromwell, shakes him and cuffs him.

HENRY *(to Cromwell)*: You! So that's your idea of a pretty woman, is it? Why I don't strike *(chokes)*. She's got a face like a *(chokes)*. And me that have never looked at *(chokes)*. What am I to do with her?

CROMWELL: I believed what I was told, sire.

HENRY: *Did* you? It's all right for you—you haven't got to marry her—I have.

CROMWELL: What would you have me
do then, Your Grace?

HENRY: Pack her back where she
came from.

CROMWELL: It would mean war, sire—
with all Europe against us.
This marriage must go on.

HENRY: All right. (*Intensely vindic-
tive*) Heaven help *you*,
Cromwell.

*He stares sombrely at Cromwell,
and strides out.*

INT.   ROYAL   BEDCHAMBER—
NIGHT

SCENE 159—FULL SHOT
*The ceremonial bed-making which
we know already. Mr. Cornell,
Mrs. Barton, the officer with the
rapier—all in depressed mood. At
last the Old Nurse appears with
her charm.*

CORNELL: The marriage-bed is made
I tell you—out you go!

NURSE: I won't, I won't!

CORNELL: I stand here for the King.

NURSE: And I stand for the Duke
of York.

CORNELL: The Duke of York?   We
have no Duke of York.

NURSE: No—but you will have,
when my charm has done
its work.

CORNELL: Oh—another charm?

NURSE: No—the same charm that gave England her Prince of Wales.

CORNELL: That was the King's doing.

NURSE: It was not! Did he get a son by his first wife? No! Did he get a son by his second wife? No! And why? Because you locked me out! (*With scathing contempt*) *You*, to stand in England's way!

INT. HENRY'S ROOM AT HAMPTON COURT—NIGHT

SCENE 160—FULL SHOT
Henry and his gentlemen of the Privy Chamber. Culpeper and Peynell among them. The gentlemen ready to help Henry for the night.

HENRY: I don't know how I'm going to go through with it! You can take a horse to water, but you cannot make him drink. I suppose it's got to be done. Give me my nightshirt.

PEYNELL (*off*): His Majesty's nightshirt!

INT. CORRIDOR AT HAMPTON COURT—NIGHT

SCENE 161—LONG SHOT

Guards in their places. A page appears with a torch in his hand. He is followed by Henry. Henry accompanied by two of his gentlemen, who will be on duty in the ante-room. The cortège goes towards the bedchamber.

INT. ROYAL BEDCHAMBER— NIGHT

SCENE 161A—CLOSE SHOT

Anne in bed. She has made herself as grotesque as possible. She makes a hideous grimace and examines the effect in her hand-mirror.

ANNE: Jah! Dat's right!

SCENE 162

Henry with his gentlemen, approaching the bedchamber. Cornell, outside the bedchamber.

CORNELL: The Royal Bedchamber is prepared.

VARIOUS UNDERLINGS: The Royal Bedchamber is prepared.

CORNELL: Rose-water!

Girls come forward with bowls of rose-water, with which they sprinkle Henry.

INT. ANTE-ROOM TO ROYAL BEDCHAMBER—NIGHT

SCENE 162A—FULL SHOT
The page stops at the door between two guards. Henry enters with his two gentlemen. He is depressed. Without a word he leaves his two gentlemen and goes into the bedchamber.

> HENRY (*with a deep sigh*): *THE THINGS I'VE DONE FOR ENGLAND!*

INT. ROYAL BEDCHAMBER—NIGHT

SCENE 163—CLOSE SHOT
Anne in bed. She listens. She hears Henry approaching. She grabs an apple from under the pillow and starts munching. Camera pans to the door. Henry enters. He stares at her with amazement and disgust. He approaches the bed and Anne.

SCENE 164—MEDIUM SHOT
Anne in the bed, Henry angrily approaching her. She sits up and shows greater anger than Henry.

> HENRY (*roaring*): Did they not give you enough to eat, Madam?

> ANNE: Don't shout at me—just because I'm your wife.

> HENRY: My wife? Not yet!

ANNE: My mother told me—first he say the marriage is not good—then he cut off the head with an axe-chopper!

HENRY: That is an exaggeration, Madam.

ANNE: Then why you say that I am not your wife?

HENRY: Why, Madam, a marriage ceremony does not make us one!

HENRY: Oh, yes, yes, I know—but —we have to——

ANNE (*off*): What?

HENRY: Oh, well, all that stuff about children being found under gooseberry bushes— that's not true.

ANNE: Oh, no—it was der shtork.

HENRY: The stork!

ANNE: Der shtork flies in der air mit der babes und down der chimney drops——

HENRY: Er—no, Madam, that isn't true either.   When a hen lays an egg, it's not entirely all her own doing.

ANNE: You mean sometimes it vas der cuckoo?

HENRY (*giving it up*): Yes—it was the cuckoo.   Do you sing?

ANNE: In Germany a respectable woman does not sing.

HENRY: Then of course you don't play?

ANNE (*off*): Oh, yes, I do.

HENRY: Good! I'll go and get you a guitar.

ANNE (*off*): No—I play cards.

HENRY: Cards? Well—that's something. I think you'll find a pack in the chest over there.

She gets the cards and throws the pack on the coverlet. They sit on the bed.

SCENE 165
Ante-room of Royal Bedchamber. Night. Culpeper and Peynell on duty. Culpeper is very cheerful, since it is not with Katherine Howard that Henry is spending the night. Peynell in the last stages of misery.

CULPEPER: Peynell, have a drink.

PEYNELL: No, thanks.

INT. ROYAL BEDCHAMBER— NIGHT

SCENE 166—CLOSE SHOT
Henry and Anne sitting on bed, preparing to play cards.

ANNE: Vot stakes shall ve play for?

HENRY: How about that?   (*Places ring on pillow.*)   Don't cry if you lose.

HENRY (*throwing Anne a card*): Good?

ANNE (*throwing Henry a card*): Better?

Anne takes his money.

HENRY: Beginner's luck!

ANNE: Stakes?

Henry throws more money on the quilt.

Don't cry if you lose!

HENRY: You may not know it, Madam, but I am considered the best card-player in England.

INT. ANTE-ROOM—NIGHT

SCENE 177

Henry suddenly appears in the doorway.

HENRY: Anybody got any money? Don't you understand the King's English? *I—NEED —MONEY!* How much was it?

ANNE (*off*): Ninety-five crowns.

HENRY (*off. To Cornell*): You! Run to the Treasury and get some money.

He returns to the bed.

HENRY: Your deal.

ANNE: Aren't you getting some money?

HENRY: Can't you give me five minutes' credit?

ANNE: I play for cash.

HENRY: *Where's that money?*

A knock.

Come in.

Cornell enters with a bag of money. Henry snatches it.

Give me that money.   Get out of here!

Cornell flies out.

(*to Anne*): Now!

Suddenly he seizes her wrist.

Cheating!

ANNE: Don't shout!

HENRY: I'm not shouting!

ANNE: You *are*!

HENRY: W—w—what am I going to do with you?

ANNE: Chop my head?

HENRY: Probably.

ANNE: You daren't!

HENRY: Why not?

ANNE: Because in Europe I vill make such a scandal as you neffer heard! It is not der first time that you chop der head. Henry der vife-butcher, that's what they shall call you!

HENRY: I don't care what they say.

I'm not going to live with you.

ANNE (*off*): Then why don't you divorce me like a chentleman?

HENRY: Did you say divorce?

ANNE: I said divorce.

HENRY: Would you consent to a divorce?

ANNE (*off*): I would consent to a divorce.

HENRY: You're a very reasonable woman.   What are your terms?

ANNE (*off*): Two manors——

HENRY: Granted.

ANNE (*off*): Richmond and Bletchingley—mit properties.

HENRY: Granted.

ANNE (*off*): Four thousand crowns a year.

HENRY: Granted.

ANNE: Annulment of the marriage on the basis of the canonic law; I leave you as a maid.

HENRY: Granted.

ANNE: Without blemish.

HENRY: Of course.

ANNE (*off*): One of your gentlemen as master of my household.

HENRY: Take whom you want.

ANNE: Peynell.

HENRY: Peynell?

ANNE: Peynell.

HENRY: Granted.   Is it a bargain?

ANNE: Ja.

HENRY: Confess, now, that you cheated, or you go back to Germany.

ANNE: Back to Germany? I cheated.

HENRY: Ah!

ANNE: Confess, though, that *you* cheated!

HENRY: What do you mean?

ANNE: Did you not hide a Katherine Howard to play against my queen?

HENRY: Oh, you knew about that?

ANNE (*off*): Ja!

HENRY: It'll only mean another scandal. At last I've found a woman I could be faithful to, but after your divorce they'll never consent to another marriage.

ANNE: Oh, yes, I think so, in a little time. And I will help you, no?

HENRY: You're the nicest girl I never married. Good night!

ANNE: Gute nacht!

Fade-out

INT. A ROOM AT HAMPTON
COURT

SCENE 178
Henry being shaved.

BARBER: Lovely weather for the time
of year, Your Grace. Will
Your Grace be pleased to
be shaved, Your Grace?

HENRY: All right. . . . Do you re-
member telling me that my
loyal Guild of Barbers
thought I ought to marry
again?

BARBER: Oh, forgive me, Your
Grace. We took a very
great liberty, Your Grace!

HENRY: Not at all—a very natural
interest in the welfare of
the country.

BARBER: You are too kind, Your
Grace.

HENRY: Are they still of the same
opinion?

BARBER: Oh, indeed, no, Your
Grace. They have realized
their mistake.

HENRY: But *was* it a mistake?

BARBER: Oh, *yes*, Your Grace! As I
said at our last meeting:
'God knows the King has
done his best to get more
sons, but there comes a
time when the well runs
dry——'

HENRY: You said that, did you?

BARBER: I did, Your Grace!

HENRY: GET OUT!

Henry jumps up in a rage. As in a previous scene he scatters the shaving materials all over the room. The barber flies.

HENRY: 'The well runs dry!'

INT. ROYAL KITCHENS

SCENE 179

A page brings in a rejected dish.

PAGE: No good! He won't touch it!

WENCH: Why, whatever's wrong?

PAGE: Everything.   Just sits and glares.

COOK: They're not trying to make him marry *again*?

CARVER: I'd like to see them, after that German business.

WOMAN: After all, you can't say he hasn't *tried*!

WIFE: Tried too often, if you ask me, to say nothing of the side dishes—a little bit of this and a little bit of that! What a man wants is regular meals.

COOK: Yes, but not the same joint every night!

WIFE: Oh!

COOK: A man loses his appetite after *four courses*.

WOMAN: How do you mean—'four courses'?

COOK: He got into the soup with Catherine of Aragon, cried stinking fish with Anne Boleyn, cooked Jane Seymour's goose, and gave Anne of Cleves the cold shoulder!

WIFE: God save him!   It's no wonder he suffers in the legs.

INT. THE GREAT HALL—NIGHT

SCENE 180—MEDIUM SHOT

Henry and his Court at dinner. He is very sulky.   He is flanked by Norfolk and Wriothesly. Cromwell is no longer present.

NORFOLK: Your grace is sad to-night. What can we do to cheer Your Grace?

HENRY: What could you do to cheer my loneliness?

NORFOLK: Your Grace is lonely?

WRIOTHESLY: That is the penalty of greatness, sire.

HENRY: Greatness!   I would exchange it all to be my lowest groom who sleeps above the stable with a wife who loves him.

Henry's eyes constantly stray to where Katherine sits. At last Norfolk and Wriothesly see what is the matter. Norfolk promptly acts on it.

NORFOLK: Your Grace, there is one matter—one most urgent matter — (*off*) — I would have waited for a happier moment, but it is so pressing. . . .

HENRY: What is it?

NORFOLK: Your Grace, your whole kingdom most urgently implores you to marry again.

HENRY: No!   Should I consent it would only be put down to desires of the flesh.

WRIOTHESLY: Never, Your Grace! Your people know you too well.

HENRY: That's what I mean.

NORFOLK (*off*): Your Grace is pleased to jest — but the will of your people has always been your law.

WRIOTHESLY: And, Your Grace, to a man they want this marriage.

HENRY: I am not eager, but if all my people wish it, what can I do? At least you have my promise to think it over. Good night, my lords.

SCENE 181—FULL SHOT

Henry rises and goes to Katherine Howard. He sits beside her. Tactfully Norfolk and Wriothesly start a general exodus.

HENRY: Little Katherine! Do you know my country is demanding a great sacrifice of me?

KATHERINE: What is it, Your Grace?

HENRY: The Lords, the Commons, the Bishops, the butcher, the baker, the candlestick-maker—even my loyal Guild of Barbers—implore me to marry again.

KATHERINE: Really? Will it be the French princess?

HENRY: No.

KATHERINE: The Emperor's niece?

HENRY: No. An English girl—if she loves me. Does she, sweetheart?

Fade-in

TITLE 2

The fifth marriage looked like a success. Katherine was happy with her crowning; Henry was happy with his Katherine.

Fade-out

INT. GREAT HALL—NIGHT

SCENE 182

Games are being held in Katherine's honour. A cockfight is in progress. A black and a red bird are fighting ferociously.

KATHERINE: The red!

HENRY: The black!

KATHERINE: The red!

HENRY: The black! Your favourite's doomed.

KATHERINE: No, no! I bet another five crowns on him. Red! Come on! Red! Ruined! You've won my last crown; I can't bet any more.

She sinks back, bitterly disappointed as her bird is beaten.

HENRY: Here, darling—and here! No matter what you lose you still have everything— me and all England.

HENRY: Take it away! Are you a better judge of men than of birds, little Kate?

Two wrestlers enter the Great Hall.

KATHERINE: Ten crowns on the taller of the two. He must be the strongest man in all England.

HENRY: All but one. The strongest man in England sits beside you!

KATHERINE: Of course, darling, I know —you have thrown every wrestler in your time.

HENRY (*nettled*): In — my — time! Hey there! Stop! Thomas! You know that a wrestler who does not pit his whole strength against his man is punished with thirty lashes of the whip?

WRESTLER: I know, Your Grace.

HENRY: Let's go.

They start wrestling. The Court looks on spellbound.

WRIOTHESLY: Good work!

NORFOLK: *Hard* work, when a man of fifty wants to show his wife he's no more than thirty.

WRIOTHESLY: He *will* show it.

SCENE 183—LONG SHOT
Henry and the wrestler. The fight at its highest pitch. Henry throws his opponent.

6

SCENE 184—FULL SHOT

The whole room is in an uproar, madly cheering the King. Henry rises, pats the vanquished wrestler on the shoulder, and amidst the madly cheering crowd steps towards Katherine.

SCENE 185—MEDIUM SHOT

Henry is approaching Katherine, while Katherine goes forward to greet him.   Henry is smiling. Suddenly he grips at his heart. He has a fainting spell.   Some gentlemen rush to him, Culpeper the first among them.

SCENE 186—LONG SHOT

Gentlemen and ladies are rushing towards Henry, who cannot be seen in this shot. Katherine is on her feet, dismayed and anxious.

KATHERINE: Send for Doctor Butts!

SCENE 187—MEDIUM SHOT

Back to Henry.   With a tremendous effort he pulls himself together.

HENRY *(halting)*: No need . . . for Dr. Butts . . . (*To Katherine*) Some air!   (*Leaning on Culpeper's arm*) Come on, Tom.   (*To Katherine*) The games go on.

Exit Henry slowly.

SCENE 188—LONG SHOT

Henry is leaning heavily on Culpeper's arm. The rest of the party remain, embarrassed.

KATHERINE (*trembling*): The games go on!

All bustle to their places.

INT. ROYAL BEDCHAMBER— NIGHT

SCENE 189—FULL SHOT

Henry is coming in with Culpeper. Henry drags himself painfully to the bed and sinks into it.

SCENE 190—MEDIUM SHOT

Culpeper and Henry. Culpeper is arranging pillows, etc. He is ready to tend Henry's leg.

CULPEPER: The leg again, sir?

Henry waving for him to leave the leg.

HENRY (*near fainting*): The head.

Henry is near fainting.

HENRY (*in a whisper*): A . . . little rest. . . . Nobody must come . . .

Culpeper arranges coverlet, the hangings, etc. . . . Henry closes his eyes. . . . Culpeper sits on the bed. . . . He looks up, and rises to stop some one entering.

SCENE 191—MEDIUM SHOT
*Camera shooting towards the door.
Katherine enters. Camera pans to
Culpeper, who tries to tell her
silently that nobody is allowed to
enter. Katherine enters the picture.
She indicates that she has the right
to be here. Culpeper dares not pro-
test any further.*

SCENE 192—MEDIUM SHOT
*Culpeper and Katherine are on
opposite sides of the bed. They
look at Henry. Then their eyes
meet. Both are shocked and
ashamed.   Katherine lowers her
head and there are tears in her eyes.*

SCENE 193—CLOSE SHOT
*Henry opens his eyes.   He sees
Katherine and tries to smile.*

HENRY: Go . . . A little rest . . .

*With a faint gesture, he indicates
that Culpeper is to draw the bed-
curtains.*

SCENE 194—MEDIUM SHOT
*Culpeper draws the bed-curtains.
Both he and Katherine withdraw a
little.*

SCENE 195—MEDIUM SHOT
*Culpeper and Katherine are in front
of the bed. They look at each
other. They hesitate, not knowing
how to begin.*

SCENE 196—CLOSE SHOT

Katherine and Culpeper. Katherine fights to hold back her tears.

> KATHERINE: Thomas!
>
> CULPEPER *(referring to Henry)*: Only a passing weakness. Don't take it so much to heart, Your Grace.
>
> KATHERINE: Have you no pity for *me*, Tom?
>
> CULPEPER *(bitterly)*: You wear the Crown.
>
> KATHERINE: What have I done with my life? I can't go on with it —I can't.
>
> CULPEPER: You must.
>
> KATHERINE: Love is everything in the world, Tom!
>
> CULPEPER: Not now. Katherine, don't! Katherine, don't!

He tries to console her. She clings to him. His self-control breaks down. She sobs bitterly. They embrace and kiss passionately.

SCENE 197—OUT

SCENE 198—MEDIUM SHOT

Katherine and Culpeper are embracing and kissing.

> HENRY *(off)*: Kate——

Culpeper and Katherine hurriedly separate. Katherine goes to the bed. Henry is parting the curtains.

SCENE 199—MEDIUM SHOT

HENRY (*off*): Kate! It was nothing, darling! You lost again! I threw your champion!

He draws Katherine to him, then looks at Culpeper. Henry waves him away.

THOMAS! Thomas, good night!

VOICE (*off*): Midnight, and all's well.

Fade-in

TITLE 3

> Every month that passed
> made life more unbearable
> for Culpeper.

Fade-out

INT. CULPEPER'S ROOM AT
HAMPTON COURT—DAY

SCENE 200—FULL SHOT
*Culpeper and his friend Paston, one
of the King's gentlemen of the
Privy Chamber, in the room. Culpeper is packing a small box with
his clothes.*

> CULPEPER *(answering a question)*: Three
> ships and a charter from
> the King.

Paston approaches him.

> PASTON: But where do you want to
> go?

SCENE 201—MEDIUM SHOT
*Culpeper ceases his activity for a
moment and looks up at his friend.*

> CULPEPER: America.
> PASTON *(sincerely amazed)*: The
> Portuguese and the Span-
> iards have grabbed it.
> CULPEPER: North America.

*He looks up at his friend defiantly.
Paston answers with a roar of
laughter.*

PASTON: North America!   It's impossible—nothing but a howling wilderness: full of howling savages!

*They are interrupted by a knock on
the door. They look out of the
picture.*

SCENE 202—MEDIUM SHOT
*Camera shooting towards the door.
Lady Rochford slips in and stands
hesitatingly as she discovers Paston.*

LADY ROCHFORD: Thomas!

*At her signal, Culpeper follows her
outside the room. Stairhead outside
Culpeper's room.*

SCENE 203—MEDIUM SHOT
*Lady Rochford with great caution.
Makes sure that there is nobody to
watch them.*

CULPEPER: When?

LADY ROCHFORD: Eleven to-night.

CULPEPER: The King?

LADY ROCHFORD: The King has just sent word not to expect him.

CULPEPER: Where?

LADY ROCHFORD: In her room—I will take you to her.

INT. STAIRCASE—NIGHT

SCENE 204—MEDIUM SHOT
Lady Rochford conducting Cul-
peper.   They hurry through this
dark portion of the corridor.

INT. QUEEN'S ROOM—NIGHT

SCENE 205—FULL SHOT
Katherine in her nightgown. She
is waiting excitedly and impatiently
for Lady Rochford and Culpeper.
The door is opened hurriedly and
cautiously.   Lady Rochford brings
in Culpeper. She indicates that she
is going to keep watch in this room
and that they ought to go into the
small room adjoining.   Katherine
and Culpeper go.

INT. SMALL ROOM NEAR THE
    QUEEN'S ROOM—NIGHT

SCENE 206—MEDIUM SHOT
Katherine enters with Culpeper.
She stops and turns.   They look at
one another.

SCENE 207—CLOSE SHOT
Katherine and Culpeper.   Kather-
ine covers her face with her hands.
They talk in whispers.

KATHERINE: I thought you were never
coming!

CULPEPER: I never *should* have come,

Kate. We can't go on like this.

KATHERINE: I know. It's dreadful— seeing each other every day and never being alone together.

Culpeper agrees in mute torture.

CULPEPER: It's being torn in half between you and the King.

KATHERINE: But, Tom, we belong to each other.

CULPEPER: No, we belong to him. Don't you realize what I'm feeling, Kate?

KATHERINE: For the King, yes. But for me, what?

CULPEPER: For you? Have you ever stood on the edge of a cliff and looked over? It draws you—*tugs* at you to hurl yourself down. You know if you look again you're gone. . . . Are you asking me to look again? Kate, are you?

KATHERINE: Then this means good-bye?

CULPEPER: It's the only way. Good-bye, Kate.

KATHERINE: Good-bye.

CULPEPER: Good-bye.

Instead of parting, it is once more an embrace and a long kiss.

INT. CORRIDOR IN FRONT OF
    PRIVY COUNCIL CHAMBER—
    NIGHT

SCENE 208—LONG SHOT
*The door to the Privy Council is
opened. Henry comes out, followed
by Cranmer, Wriothesly and other
members of the Privy Council,
together with the French and German ambassadors. Henry tired and
sleepy, but very happy.   They
approach the camera.*

> HENRY: Good night, gentlemen.
> GENTLEMEN: Good night, Your Majesty.

*Henry takes Cranmer by the arm.
He is in a communicative mood and
wants to say a few words to him.*

SCENE 209—MEDIUM SHOT
*Henry with Cranmer. Before he
speaks, Henry turns suddenly and
calls:*

> HENRY: Wriothesly!

Wriothesly enters the picture.

> HENRY: Wriothesly!   Sir Thomas
> Wyatt is in the Tower.
> He wrote beautiful love
> poems.   Send word that
> they release him.
>
> WRIOTHESLY: Yes, Your Grace.
> HENRY: And cancel all death sen-
> tences.
> WRIOTHESLY: Yes, Your Grace.
> HENRY: Good night, gentlemen.
> ALL: Good night, Your Majesty.

He dismisses Wriothesly with a friendly gesture. And now he talks to Cranmer.

HENRY: Through how many blunders, stupidities, and cruelties has a man to pass before he finds his happiness in a wife.

CRANMER: We thank God that He has given Your Majesty this happiness at last.

HENRY: Love is drunkenness when one is young. Love is wisdom at my age. Life has found its meaning, Cranmer. Good night.

CRANMER: Good night, Your Majesty.

He goes. Cranmer bows and turns to the other gentlemen in the background.

INT. SMALL ROOM NEAR THE QUEEN'S ROOM—NIGHT

SCENE 210—MEDIUM SHOT
Katherine and Culpeper. They are once more in an embrace. They break away.

KATHERINE: Take me with you, Tom!

CULPEPER: Where could we go? His arm would reach us everywhere.

CULPEPER: Good-bye, Kate.

KATHERINE *(a desperate outcry)*: Shall I never see you again, Tom?

Culpeper answers with a gesture
that is cruel for himself as well.

Take me with you.

She clings to him, Culpeper looks
down at her hopelessly.

CULPEPER: Where could we go? His
arm would reach us every-
where. Good-bye, Kate.

Katherine stammers a good-bye, but
she stammers the words again with
her lips to Culpeper's.   The door
is flung open and Lady Rochford
hurries in.

LADY ROCHFORD: Katherine!   Katherine!
The King is coming.

Katherine and Culpeper so paralysed
by fear that they cannot break away
or do anything.   Lady Rochford
grips Katherine's hand and drags
her towards the other room.   They
have only time to signal to Culpeper
to stay where he is and not to stir.
They hurry out.

INT. QUEEN'S ROOM—NIGHT

SCENE 211—FULL SHOT
Katherine and Lady Rochford
hurry in from the small room.
Directed by Lady Rochford, Kather-
ine throws down her nightgown and
slips into the bed.   No sooner is she
in bed than a knock is heard on the
door.   Lady Rochford flies towards
the door, casting a last look round
the room.

SCENE 212—MEDIUM SHOT

Lady Rochford opens the door. Henry enters. Lady Rochford bows and Henry dismisses her with a friendly gesture. Lady Rochford goes, after a look of terror towards Katherine and the door to the small room. Henry approaches the bed.

SCENE 213—MEDIUM SHOT

Katherine in the bed. Henry entering the picture and sitting on the bed. He kisses her hand. He embraces her tenderly.

INT. SMALL ROOM NEAR THE QUEEN'S ROOM—NIGHT

SCENE 214—CLOSE SHOT

Culpeper in the darkness—alone—listening—trembling with fear for his life, and fear that he will be the witness of a love-scene.

INT. QUEEN'S ROOM—NIGHT

Henry and Katherine.

HENRY: My little Katherine! More and more charming every day. You know, I couldn't resist coming to see you. . . . (*Off*) Do you know that the Emperor offers me half France if I join him? . . . And the French offer me Flanders. They're very generous with each other's territory. In my youth, in Wolsey's time, I would have accepted one offer or the other. But what is the use of new territories and wars, wars, wars? If these French and Germans don't stop killing one another the whole of Europe will be in ruins. I want to compel them to keep peace, peace, peace—and there's nobody in Europe to help me. . . . My little girl! I'm boring you with business and you are tired. You are very sleepy and so am I. Sleep well, darling. Good night. Sleep well.

He kisses her forehead and goes out.

SCENE 215—FULL SHOT

Exit Henry. Katherine stares after him. She hesitates. She is unable to come to any decision. The door of the small room opens. Culpeper enters. Katherine extends her arm as if to stop him. Culpeper comes to the bed.

SCENE 216—CLOSE SHOT

Culpeper sits on the bed. They stare at each other. Katherine sits

*up in the bed.   She reaches for a
candle near the bed and blows it
out.   They embrace.*

SCENE 217—FLASHES

*Yeomen blowing out candles in
several parts of the palace.   Guards
on duty beginning the half sleep of
the watch.*

EXT. COURTYARD—NIGHT

SCENE 218—LONG SHOT

*The watch making its round
through the courtyards of the
palace.   A lantern in the leader's
hand.   They approach the camera.*

LEADER: It is midnight.   All is well.

Fade-out

Fade-in

INT. ROOM AT HAMPTON COURT
    —DAY

SCENE 219—MEDIUM SHOT

*Cranmer and Wriothesly in the
room.   Cranmer desperate, Wriothesly hard as steel.   The door
opens and a yeoman conducts Lady
Rochford into the room.   Wriothesly
signals to the yeoman to go.   Lady
Rochford smiling.   Wriothesly approaches her.*

SCENE 220—CLOSE SHOT

Lady Rochford and Wriothesly.
Lady Rochford slowly ceases to
smile as she stares into Wrio-
thesly's face.

> WRIOTHESLY: Lady Rochford—do you know what it means to be put on the rack?

Lady Rochford answers with a
scream.

> Your bones will be broken piece by piece.

Lady Rochford begins to cry.

> Wouldn't you rather tell us everything you know about the Queen—and Thomas Culpeper.

Lady Rochford cries. Wriothesly
shakes her.

> LADY ROCHFORD: The rack—or confess——
> (*With a scream*) Not the rack!

SCENE 221—MEDIUM SHOT

Wriothesly sits down to write Lady
Rochford's confession. Cranmer in
deep sorrow.   Lady Rochford
trembling in front of them.

> WRIOTHESLY: You conducted him to the Queen the first time— when?

> LADY ROCHFORD: Six months ago.

Wriothesly writes.

7

INT. GREAT HALL—DAY

SCENE 222—LONG SHOT

Dance in progress.   Katherine taking no part in the dance. Henry, sitting in a sort of throne-chair, enjoys the sight. Culpeper, at the wall, is watching Katherine. Henry is sitting contentedly sipping his wine.

HENRY: What's the matter with all you young people? Katherine, why aren't you dancing?

KATHERINE: You said you didn't want to dance.

SCENE 223—MEDIUM SHOT

Katherine and Culpeper dancing.

KATHERINE (*whispering*): Darling!

CULPEPER: What?

KATHERINE: I adore you!

Culpeper answers with an adoring look.

INT. ROOM OF PRIVY COUNCIL —DAY

SCENE 224—FULL SHOT

The Privy Council gathered. Everybody knows already what is in preparation.   Everybody shuddering a little.

SCENE 225—MEDIUM SHOT

Wriothesly and Cranmer.   Cranmer in despair.

> WRIOTHESLY (*to Cranmer*): My lord, only you can tell His Majesty. You must tell him.

> CRANMER: I can't.

SCENE 225A

Henry sipping his wine. A Gentleman-usher enters. Henry rises. He waves farewell to Katherine.

> USHER: Your Majesty's Privy Council awaits Your Majesty's orders.

> HENRY: Forgive me, darling—affairs of state. (The dance goes on.)

SCENE 226—FULL SHOT

The Privy Council. Henry entering.

> HENRY (*very genial*): Good evening, gentlemen.

He goes to his place, patting a shoulder here and a back there as he goes. He sits. Everybody sits.

SCENE 227—MEDIUM SHOT

Henry and his neighbours.

> HENRY: Well—anything important? I can't be long—(*with a smile*)—the Queen is waiting for me.

Silence round the table.

> HENRY (*a little surprised, to Wriothesly*): Well, Mr. Secretary?

7*

WRIOTHESLY (*with great exertion*): His Lordship, the Archbishop of Canterbury has an important matter to submit to Your Majesty.

CRANMER: Your Majesty—er——

Henry interrogatively turning to Cranmer.

HENRY: Come along, Cranmer.

CRANMER (*tears in his eyes*): Your Majesty—history teaches —even the Scriptures tell us—that—that——

HENRY: What is it?

CRANMER: —bad women of all times —even those who wore crowns——

He cannot continue, because Henry slowly understands and rises with his hands raised. Cranmer collapses. Henry shakes him. Cranmer is unable to continue. Henry looks round.

HENRY: What is it? (*More loudly*) What is it?

Nobody dares to say a word.

(*Furiously*): WHAT IS IT?

Wriothesly with cold courage.

WRIOTHESLY: His Lordship was trying to fulfil the most painful duty of a loyal subject: to tell the King that the Queen has committed adultery.

*Henry panting. He slowly puts his
two hands round Wriothesly's neck
as if to kill him.*

HENRY: With whom?

WRIOTHESLY: With Thomas Culpeper.

*Henry strengthens his grip round
Wriothesly's neck.*

WRIOTHESLY *(choking)*: It is proved,
Your Majesty—there are
witnesses.

The witnesses are Lady
Rochford, three maids of
the Queen, John Cornell,
the ladies Parnell, Bassett
and Morton, the Queen's
two pages and Culpeper's
body servant.

*Henry looks at the faces round the
table.   He searches for something
that can allow some doubt.   He
does not find anything. He turns
back towards the garden, as if he
wanted to go and kill at once the
young people outside.   He gives it
up; he turns back to his Council,
breaks down, falls into his chair.
He tries to give an order, to say
something.   He cannot.   He puts
his head on his arms and weeps.
The members of the Council
deeply moved.*

SCENE 228—CLOSE SHOT
*Henry with his head on his arms.
His shoulders shaking.*

Dissolve

INT. THE GREAT HALL

SCENE 228A—CLOSE SHOT
Culpeper and Katherine are dancing.

CULPEPER: Katherine!   Why is there a Council to-night?

KATHERINE: The French and the Germans again, I suppose. Who cares?

SCENE 229—CLOSE SHOT
Henry in another dress, in another room, but with his head on his arms. He lifts his head as if to listen to something.

EXT. TOWER GREEN—DAY

SCENE 230—FULL SHOT
Everything ready for the execution: scaffold, block, executioner.   The spectators in breathless silence watching the cortège coming out of the Tower.   It is the same arrangement as with Anne Boleyn.   The cortège reaches the scaffold.

SCENE 231—MEDIUM SHOT
Katherine on the scaffold.   She tries to talk and she succeeds with suppressed sobs.

KATHERINE: I die a Queen—I would rather die as the wife of the

> man I loved and who died
> for me—greed of grandeur
> blinded me——

*She cannot continue. She sobs.
Her ladies try to comfort her. She
pulls herself together.*

SCENE 232—CLOSE SHOT
Katherine and the Executioner.

> KATHERINE (*turns to Executioner*): Pray
> hasten with your office.

*She kneels down. The headsman
raises his sword.*

SCENE 233—DETAIL SHOT
A gun being fired.

INT. ROOM AT HAMPTON
COURT—DAY

SCENE 234—MEDIUM SHOT
*Henry sitting with his head on his
arms. He hears the report of the
gun. With a sudden jerk he raises
his head and raises his hands, as if
he wanted to arrest the wheels of fate
—A picture of utter sorrow and
pain.*

> HENRY: Katherine! . . . *Katherine!*
> . . . Mea culpa! Mea
> maxima culpa!

SCENE 235

Fade-in

TITLE 4   A.D. 1543

INT. A ROOM OVERLOOKING
  THE GARDENS AT HAMPTON
  COURT

SCENE 236—CLOSE SHOT
*Henry seated at a table, alone and
weary. A knock at the door.*

           HENRY: Yes?

Wriothesly enters.

   WRIOTHESLY: Your Grace——

          HENRY: Go away! I'm tired—no
                more business to-day.

   WRIOTHESLY: This is not business, Your
                Grace. The Lady Anne is
                asking for an audience.

          HENRY (*puzzled*): Anne? Anne?

   WRIOTHESLY: The Lady Anne of Cleves.

          HENRY: Ha! Anne! Tell her to
                come in.

*Wriothesly bows and opens the door
for Anne, who comes forward as
Wriothesly goes out.*

          HENRY: Well, well, well!

           ANNE: Good morning, Your High-
                ness!

          HENRY: Good morning, Your High-
                ness!

           ANNE: Well? How's life?

          HENRY: Oh, it's rather sad, Anne.

ANNE: But why?

HENRY: I haven't any friends. I haven't any wife, there's no love in my life—I've nothing left, not even hatred.

ANNE: What you need is a good wife.

Henry waves the suggestion aside.

ANNE: I said a *good* wife. Not a spiteful one, like the first. Not an ambitious one, like the second. Not a stupid one, like the third——

HENRY (*slyly*): Not a card-sharper, like the fourth——

ANNE: No, and not a very young one, like the fifth. I said, a *good* one.

HENRY: Where do you find 'em?

ANNE: I'll show you!

Anne takes him to the window, whence they look down into the garden.

EXT. THE GARDENS, HAMPTON COURT

SCENE 237—LONG SHOT
Henry's children, Edward and Elizabeth, with their nurse. Katherine Parr comes into the picture. She is greeted by delighted shouts from the children.

CHILDREN: Katherine! Katherine!

They run excitedly to Katherine.
She at once notices that Edward
has a dirty face.

KATHERINE: Oh, nurse! Don't you *see*?

Katherine gets out a handkerchief.

KATHERINE: Blow, darling!

Edward dutifully blows. Katherine
kisses him.

ELIZABETH: Me, too!

KATHERINE: But your face is quite clean, Elizabeth!

ELIZABETH (*insistently*): Me, too!

Katherine realizes that Elizabeth
wants a kiss. She gives her one.

KATHERINE: You too, darling.

INT. HENRY'S ROOM

SCENE 238—CLOSE SHOT
Henry and Anne at the window.

HENRY: I know her.

ANNE: Katherine Parr.

Henry winces. The name of Kath-
erine awakes memories.

HENRY: Katherine. Katherine . . .

INT. A ROOM IN THE PALACE

SCENE 239—CLOSE SHOT
Henry and Katherine Parr are
seated at a table before the fire.
Henry is ageing fast and becoming
rather shaky, but still takes a very
hearty interest in his food. He

*picks up a large fragment of meat
and attacks it with gusto.*

KATHERINE: *No,* Henry!

*Henry surreptitiously continues to
gobble while she nags at him.*

KATHERINE: I don't know what I'm
going to do with you! If I
let you out of my sight for
five minutes you're up to
some mischief!

Yesterday, when I turned
my back on you for a
moment, you ate a whole
saddle of mutton. And who
had to nurse you when you
had the belly-ache all night
long? *Me!*

*She arrests him in the act of trans-
ferring another large helping to his
mouth.*

Now, *Henry*! You know
you can't digest it!

Katherine calls up the servants.

KATHERINE: Take it away! *And* the
drink.

*She waves a comprehensive hand.
The servants hesitate.*

HENRY (*angrily*): Don't you hear
what the Queen says? Take
it away!

*The servants remove the viands,
placing some of them on a side
table.*

KATHERINE: And bring a blanket.

She pushes Henry's chair nearer the fire, takes a blanket from the servant, and fusses round Henry— tucking him up and making him cosy.

KATHERINE: Now for a little nap!

She gives the blanket a final pat and waits to see Henry close his eyes. Then she steals softly out of the picture. . . .

. . . Henry leans back, with closed eyes. Apparently he has dozed off. Actually he is listening intently for Katherine's footsteps to die away.

After a few moments he very cautiously opens one eye. The coast is clear. He makes quite sure of this, and then, with a spark of the old vigour, he kicks off the blanket, rises and shuffles off to the side-table, where he finds the treasured haunch of venison.

With twinkling eyes, and ears alert to catch the slightest movement on the part of the enemy, he attacks the succulent morsel.

HENRY *(with his mouth full)*: Six wives—and the best of them's the worst!

Jarrold & Sons, Ltd., The Empire Press, Norwich

METHUEN'S
GENERAL LITERATURE

A SELECTION OF
MESSRS. METHUEN'S PUBLICATIONS

This Catalogue contains only a selection of the more important books published by Messrs. Methuen. A complete catalogue of their publications may be obtained on application.

ABRAHAM (G. D.)
MODERN MOUNTAINEERING
Illustrated. 7s. 6d. net.

ARMSTRONG (Anthony) ('A. A.' of Punch)
WARRIORS AT EASE
WARRIORS STILL AT EASE
SELECTED WARRIORS
PERCIVAL AND I
PERCIVAL AT PLAY
APPLE AND PERCIVAL
ME AND FRANCES
HOW TO DO IT
BRITISHER ON BROADWAY
WHILE YOU WAIT
Each 3s. 6d. net.
LIVESTOCK IN BARRACKS
Illustrated by E. H. SHEPARD.
3s. 6d. net.
EASY WARRIORS
Illustrated by G. L. STAMPA.
5s. net.
YESTERDAILIES. Illustrated.
3s. 6d. net.

BADEN-POWELL OF GILWELL (Lord)
INCIDENTS AND ACCIDENTS.
Illustrated. 5s. net.

BALFOUR (Sir Graham)
THE LIFE OF ROBERT LOUIS STEVENSON 10s. 6d. net.
Also, 3s. 6d. net.

BARKER (Ernest)
NATIONAL CHARACTER
10s. 6d. net.
GREEK POLITICAL THEORY 14s. net.
CHURCH, STATE AND STUDY
10s. 6d. net.

BELLOC (Hilaire)
PARIS 8s. 6d. net.
THE PYRENEES 8s. 6d. net.
MARIE ANTOINETTE 18s. net.
A HISTORY OF ENGLAND
In 7 Vols. Vols. I, II, III and IV
Each 15s. net.

BINNS (L. Elliott), D.D.
THE DECLINE AND FALL OF THE MEDIEVAL PAPACY. 16s. net.

BIRMINGHAM (George A.)
A WAYFARER IN HUNGARY
Illustrated. 8s. 6d. net.
SPILLIKINS : ESSAYS 3s. 6d. net.
SHIPS AND SEALING-WAX : ESSAYS
3s. 6d. net.
CAN I BE A CHRISTIAN ? 1s. net.

CANE (Percy S.)
GARDEN DESIGN OF TO-DAY.
Illustrated. 15s. net.

CASTLEROSSE (Viscount)
VALENTINE'S DAYS
Illustrated. 12s. 6d. net.

CHALMERS (Patrick R.)
KENNETH GRAHAME : LIFE, LETTERS AND UNPUBLISHED WORK
Illustrated. 10s. 6d. net.

CHESTERTON (G. K.)
COLLECTED POEMS 7s. 6d. net.
THE BALLAD OF THE WHITE HORSE
3s. 6d. net.
Also illustrated by ROBERT AUSTIN. 12s. 6d. net

CHESTERTON (G. K.)—*continued*
AVOWALS AND DENIALS   *6s. net.*
ALL I SURVEY
ALL IS GRIST
CHARLES DICKENS
COME TO THINK OF IT . . .
GENERALLY SPEAKING
ALL THINGS CONSIDERED
TREMENDOUS TRIFLES
FANCIES VERSUS FADS
ALARMS AND DISCURSIONS
A MISCELLANY OF MEN
THE USES OF DIVERSITY
THE OUTLINE OF SANITY
THE FLYING INN
         Each 3s. 6d. net.
WINE, WATER AND SONG 1s. 6d. net.

CURLE (J. H.)
THE SHADOW-SHOW   *6s. net.*
        Also, *3s. 6d. net.*
THIS WORLD OF OURS   *6s. net.*
TO-DAY AND TO-MORROW   *6s. net.*
THIS WORLD FIRST   *6s. net.*

EDWARDES (Tickner)
THE LORE OF THE HONEY-BEE
Illustrated. 7s. 6d. and 3s. 6d. net.
BEE-KEEPING FOR ALL
      Illustrated. *3s. 6d. net.*
THE BEE-MASTER OF WARRILOW
      Illustrated. *7s. 6d. net.*
BEE-KEEPING DO'S AND DON'TS
         2s. 6d. net.
LIFT-LUCK ON SOUTHERN ROADS
         5s. net.

EINSTEIN (Albert)
RELATIVITY : THE SPECIAL AND
   GENERAL THEORY   *5s. net.*
SIDELIGHTS ON RELATIVITY
         3s. 6d. net.
THE MEANING OF RELATIVITY
         5s. net.
THE BROWNIAN MOVEMENT
         5s. net.

EISLER (Robert)
THE MESSIAH JESUS AND JOHN THE
BAPTIST
      Illustrated. £2 *2s. net.*

FINER (H.)
THE THEORY AND PRACTICE OF
MODERN GOVERNMENT   2 vols.
         £2 *2s. net.*
ENGLISH LOCAL GOVERNMENT
         £1 *1s. net.*

FYLEMAN (Rose)
HAPPY FAMILIES
FAIRIES AND CHIMNEYS
THE FAIRY GREEN
THE FAIRY FLUTE   *Each 2s. net.*
THE RAINBOW CAT
EIGHT LITTLE PLAYS FOR CHILDREN
FORTY GOOD-NIGHT TALES
FORTY GOOD-MORNING TALES
SEVEN LITTLE PLAYS FOR CHILDREN
TWENTY TEA-TIME TALES
         Each 3s. 6d . net.
THE BLUE RHYME BOOK
      Illustrated. *3s. 6d. net.*
THE EASTER HARE
      Illustrated. *3s. 6d. net.*
FIFTY-ONE NEW NURSERY RHYMES
Illustrated by DOROTHY BUR-
ROUGHES.   *6s. net.*
THE STRANGE ADVENTURES OF
CAPTAIN MARWHOPPLE
      Illustrated. *3s. 6d. net.*

GIBBON (Edward)
THE DECLINE AND FALL OF THE
   ROMAN EMPIRE
With Notes, Appendixes and Maps,
by J. B. BURY. Illustrated. 7 vols.
15s. net each volume. Also, unillustrated, 7s. 6d. net each volume.

GOLDMAN (Bosworth)
RED ROAD THROUGH ASIA
      Illustrated. 12s. 6d. net.

GRAHAME (Kenneth)
THE WIND IN THE WILLOWS
     7s. 6d. net and 5s. net.
Also illustrated by ERNEST H.
SHEPARD. Cloth, 7s. 6d. net.
Green Leather, 12s. 6d. net.
Pocket Edition, unillustrated.
      Cloth, 3s. 6d. net.
      Green Morocco, 7s. 6d. net.
THE KENNETH GRAHAME BOOK
(' The Wind in the Willows ',
' Dream Days ' and ' The Golden
Age ' in one volume).
         7s. 6d. net.
See also Milne (A. A.)

GREGORY (T. E.)
THE GOLD STANDARD AND ITS
FUTURE   3s. 6d. net.

HALL (H. R.)
THE ANCIENT HISTORY OF THE
NEAR EAST £1 1s. net.
THE CIVILIZATION OF GREECE IN
THE BRONZE AGE £1 10s. net.

HEATON (Rose Henniker)
THE PERFECT HOSTESS
Decorated by A. E. TAYLOR.
7s. 6d. net. Gift Edition, £1 1s. net.
THE PERFECT SCHOOLGIRL
3s. 6d. net.

HEIDEN (Konrad)
A HISTORY OF NATIONAL SOCIALISM
15s. net.

HERBERT (A. P.)
HELEN 2s. 6d. net.
TANTIVY TOWERS and DERBY DAY
in one volume. Illustrated by
Lady VIOLET BARING. 5s. net.
Each, separately, unillustrated
2s. 6d. net.
HONEYBUBBLE & CO. 3s. 6d. net.
MISLEADING CASES IN THE COMMON
LAW 5s. net.
MORE MISLEADING CASES 5s. net.
STILL MORE MISLEADING CASES
5s. net.
THE WHEREFORE AND THE WHY
'TINKER, TAILOR . . .'
Each, illustrated by GEORGE
MORROW. 2s. 6d. net.
THE SECRET BATTLE 3s. 6d. net.
THE HOUSE BY THE RIVER
3s. 6d. net.
MR. PEWTER 5s. net.
'NO BOATS ON THE RIVER'
Illustrated. 5s. net.

HOLDSWORTH (Sir W. S.)
A HISTORY OF ENGLISH LAW
Nine Volumes. £1 5s. net each.
Index Volume by EDWARD POTTON.
£1 1s. net.

HSIUNG (S. I.)
LADY PRECIOUS STREAM:
An Old Chinese Play
Illustrated. 8s. 6d. net.
Limited and Signed Edition
£2 2s. net.

HUDSON (W. H.)
A SHEPHERD'S LIFE
Illustrated. 10s. 6d. net.
Also unillustrated. 3s. 6d. net.

HUTTON (Edward)
CITIES OF SICILY
Illustrated. 10s. 6d. net.
MILAN AND LOMBARDY

HUTTON (Edward)—*continued*
THE CITIES OF ROMAGNA AND THE
MARCHES
SIENA AND SOUTHERN TUSCANY
NAPLES AND SOUTHERN ITALY
Illustrated. Each 8s. 6d. net.
A WAYFARER IN UNKNOWN TUSCANY
THE CITIES OF SPAIN
THE CITIES OF UMBRIA
COUNTRY WALKS ABOUT FLORENCE
ROME
FLORENCE AND NORTHERN TUSCANY
VENICE AND VENETIA
Illustrated. Each 7s. 6d. net.

INGE (W. R.), D.D., Dean of St. Paul's
CHRISTIAN MYSTICISM. With a New
Preface. 7s. 6d. net.

JOAD (C. E. M.)
COMMON-SENSE ETHICS 6s. net.

JOHNS (Rowland)
DOGS YOU'D LIKE TO MEET
LET DOGS DELIGHT
ALL SORTS OF DOGS
LET'S TALK OF DOGS
PUPPIES
LUCKY DOGS
EVERY DOG ITS DAY
Each, Illustrated, 3s. 6d. net.
SO YOU LIKE DOGS !
NURSE CAVELL : DOG LOVER
Each, Illustrated, 2s. 6d. net.
THE ROWLAND JOHNS DOG BOOK.
Illustrated. 5s. net.

─────────────

'OUR FRIEND THE DOG' SERIES
Edited by ROWLAND JOHNS.
THE CAIRN
THE COCKER SPANIEL
THE FOX-TERRIER
THE PEKINGESE
THE AIREDALE
THE ALSATIAN
THE SCOTTISH TERRIER
THE CHOW-CHOW
THE IRISH SETTER
THE DALMATIAN
THE LABRADOR
THE SEALYHAM
THE DACHSHUND
THE BULLDOG
THE BULL-TERRIER
THE GREAT DANE
THE POMERANIAN
THE COLLIE
THE ENGLISH SPRINGER
THE HOUSE-DOG
Each 2s. 6d. net.

KIPLING (Rudyard)

BARRACK-ROOM BALLADS
THE SEVEN SEAS
THE FIVE NATIONS
DEPARTMENTAL DITTIES
THE YEARS BETWEEN

Four Editions of these famous volumes of poems are now published, viz. :—*Buckram*, 7s. 6d. net. *Cloth*, 6s. net. *Leather*, 7s. 6d. net. Service Edition. Two volumes each book. 3s. net each vol.

A KIPLING ANTHOLOGY—VERSE
    Leather, 7s. 6d. net.
    Cloth, 6s. net and 3s. 6d. net.
TWENTY POEMS FROM RUDYARD
    KIPLING   1s. net.
A CHOICE OF SONGS   2s. net.
SELECTED POEMS   1s. net.

LAMB (Charles and Mary)

THE COMPLETE WORKS
    Edited by E. V. Lucas. Six volumes.   6s. net each.
SELECTED LETTERS
    Edited by G. T. CLAPTON.
                3s. 6d. net.
THE CHARLES LAMB DAY-BOOK
    Compiled by E. V. Lucas. 6s. net.
THE LETTERS OF CHARLES LAMB
    Edited by E. V. Lucas. Two volumes.   6s. net each.
THE BEST OF LAMB
    Edited by E. V. Lucas. 2s. 6d. net.

LANKESTER (Sir Ray)

SCIENCE FROM AN EASY CHAIR
    First Series
SCIENCE FROM AN EASY CHAIR
    Second Series
GREAT AND SMALL THINGS
    Each, Illustrated, 7s. 6d. net.
SECRETS OF EARTH AND SEA
    Illustrated. 8s. 6d. net.

LENNHOFF (Eugen)

THE FREEMASONS
    Illustrated. 21s. net.

LINDRUM (Walter)

BILLIARDS. Illustrated. 2s. 6d. net.

LODGE (Sir Oliver)

MAN AND THE UNIVERSE
    7s. 6d. net and 3s. 6d. net.
THE SURVIVAL OF MAN 7s. 6d. net.
RAYMOND   10s. 6d. net.
RAYMOND REVISED   6s. net.
MODERN PROBLEMS   3s. 6d. net.
REASON AND BELIEF   3s. 6d. net.
THE SUBSTANCE OF FAITH 2s. net.
RELATIVITY   1s. net.
CONVICTION OF SURVIVAL 2s. net.

LUCAS (E. V.), C.H.

READING, WRITING AND REMEM-
    BERING   7s. 6d. net.
THE COLVINS AND THEIR FRIENDS
                £1 1s. net.
THE LIFE OF CHARLES LAMB
    2 Vols.   £1 1s. net.
AT THE SHRINE OF ST. CHARLES
                5s. net.
POST-BAG DIVERSIONS 7s. 6d. net.
VERMEER THE MAGICAL   5s. net.
A WANDERER IN ROME
A WANDERER IN HOLLAND
A WANDERER IN LONDON
LONDON REVISITED (Revised)
A WANDERER IN PARIS
A WANDERER IN FLORENCE
A WANDERER IN VENICE
    Each 10s. 6d. net.
A WANDERER AMONG PICTURES
                8s. 6d. net.
E. V. LUCAS'S LONDON   £1 net.
THE OPEN ROAD   6s. net.
Also, illustrated by CLAUDE A.
    SHEPPERSON, A.R.W.S.
                10s. 6d. net.
Also, India Paper.
    Leather, 7s. 6d. net.
THE JOY OF LIFE   6s. net.
    Leather Edition, 7s. 6d. net.
Also, India Paper.
    Leather, 7s. 6d. net.
THE GENTLEST ART
THE SECOND POST
FIRESIDE AND SUNSHINE
CHARACTER AND COMEDY
GOOD COMPANY
ONE DAY AND ANOTHER
OLD LAMPS FOR NEW
LOITERER'S HARVEST
LUCK OF THE YEAR
EVENTS AND EMBROIDERIES
A FRONDED ISLE
A ROVER I WOULD BE
GIVING AND RECEIVING
HER INFINITE VARIETY
ENCOUNTERS AND DIVERSIONS
TURNING THINGS OVER
TRAVELLER'S LUCK
AT THE SIGN OF THE DOVE
VISIBILITY GOOD
LEMON VERBENA *Each* 3s. 6d. net.
SAUNTERER'S REWARDS
                6s. net.
FRENCH LEAVES
ENGLISH LEAVES
THE BARBER'S CLOCK *Each* 5s. net.
' THE MORE I SEE OF MEN . .'

LUCAS (E. V.)—*continued*
OUT OF A CLEAR SKY
IF DOGS COULD WRITE
' . . . AND SUCH SMALL DEER '
Each 3s. 6d. net.
See also **Lamb (Charles).**

LYND (Robert)
BOTH SIDES OF THE ROAD
THE COCKLESHELL *Each* 5s. net.
RAIN, RAIN, GO TO SPAIN
IT'S A FINE WORLD
THE GREEN MAN
THE PLEASURES OF IGNORANCE
THE GOLDFISH
THE LITTLE ANGEL
THE BLUE LION
THE PEAL OF BELLS
THE ORANGE TREE
THE MONEY-BOX *Each* 3s. 6d. net.
'YY.' An Anthology of essays by
ROBERT LYND. Edited by EILEEN
SQUIRE. 7s. 6d. net.

McDOUGALL (William)
AN INTRODUCTION TO SOCIAL
PSYCHOLOGY 10s. 6d. net.
NATIONAL WELFARE AND NATIONAL
DECAY 6s. net.
AN OUTLINE OF PSYCHOLOGY
10s. 6d. net.
AN OUTLINE OF ABNORMAL PSYCHO-
LOGY 15s. net.
BODY AND MIND 12s. 6d. net.
CHARACTER AND THE CONDUCT OF
LIFE 10s. 6d. net.
MODERN MATERIALISM AND EMER-
GENT EVOLUTION 3s. 6d. net.
ETHICS AND SOME MODERN WORLD
PROBLEMS 7s. 6d. net.
THE ENERGIES OF MEN 8s. 6d. net.
RELIGION AND THE SCIENCES OF
LIFE 8s. 6d. net.

MAETERLINCK (Maurice)
THE BLUE BIRD 6s. net.
Also, illustrated by F. CAYLEY
ROBINSON. 10s. 6d. net.
OUR ETERNITY 6s. net.
THE UNKNOWN GUEST 6s. net.
POEMS 5s. net.
THE WRACK OF THE STORM 6s. net.
THE BETROTHAL 6s. net.
MARY MAGDALENE 2s. net.

MARLOWE (Christopher)
THE WORKS. In 6 volumes.
General Editor, R. H. CASE.
THE LIFE OF MARLOWE and DIDO,
QUEEN OF CARTHAGE 8s. 6d. net.
TAMBURLAINE, I AND II 10s.6d.net.

MARLOWE (Christopher)—*cont.*
THE WORKS—*continued*
THE JEW OF MALTA and THE
MASSACRE AT PARIS 10s. 6d. net.
POEMS 10s. 6d. net.
DOCTOR FAUSTUS 8s. 6d. net.
EDWARD II 8s. 6d. net.

MARTIN (William)
UNDERSTAND THE CHINESE
Illustrated. 7s. 6d. net.

MASEFIELD (John)
ON THE SPANISH MAIN 8s. 6d. net.
A SAILOR'S GARLAND 3s. 6d. net.
SEA LIFE IN NELSON'S TIME
7s. 6d. net.

METHUEN (Sir A.)
AN ANTHOLOGY OF MODERN VERSE
SHAKESPEARE TO HARDY: An
Anthology of English Lyrics.
Each, Cloth, 6s. net.
Leather, 7s. 6d. net.

MILNE (A. A.)
PEACE WITH HONOUR 5s. net.
TOAD OF TOAD HALL
A Play founded on Kenneth
Grahame's ' The Wind in the
Willows '. 5s. net.
THOSE WERE THE DAYS: Collected
Stories 7s. 6d. net.
BY WAY OF INTRODUCTION
NOT THAT IT MATTERS
IF I MAY
THE SUNNY SIDE
THE RED HOUSE MYSTERY
ONCE A WEEK
THE HOLIDAY ROUND
THE DAY'S PLAY
MR. PIM PASSES BY *Each* 3s. 6d. net.
WHEN WE WERE VERY YOUNG
WINNIE-THE-POOH
NOW WE ARE SIX
THE HOUSE AT POOH CORNER
Each illustrated by E. H. SHEPARD.
7s. 6d. net. *Leather*, 10s. 6d. net.
THE CHRISTOPHER ROBIN VERSES
('When We were Very Young'
and 'Now We are Six' com-
plete in one volume). Illustrated
in colour and line by E. H.
SHEPARD. 8s. 6d. net.
THE CHRISTOPHER ROBIN STORY
BOOK
Illustrated by E. H. SHEPARD.
5s. net.
THE CHRISTOPHER ROBIN BIRTH-
DAY BOOK
Illustrated by E. H. SHEPARD.
3s. 6d. net.

MILNE (A. A.) and FRASER-SIM-SON (H.)

FOURTEEN SONGS FROM ' WHEN WE WERE VERY YOUNG ' 7s. 6d. net.

TEDDY BEAR AND OTHER SONGS FROM ' WHEN WE WERE VERY YOUNG' 7s. 6d. net.

THE KING'S BREAKFAST 3s. 6d. net.

SONGS FROM ' NOW WE ARE SIX ' 7s. 6d. net.

MORE ' VERY YOUNG ' SONGS 7s. 6d. net.

THE HUMS OF POOH 7s. 6d. net.

In each case the words are by A. A. MILNE, the music by H. FRASER-SIMSON, and the decorations by E. H. SHEPARD.

MITCHELL (Abe)

DOWN TO SCRATCH 5s. net.

MORTON (H. V.)

A LONDON YEAR Illustrated, 6s. net.

THE HEART OF LONDON 3s. 6d. net.

Also, with Scissor Cuts by L. HUMMEL. 6s. net.

THE SPELL OF LONDON

THE NIGHTS OF LONDON

BLUE DAYS AT SEA Each 3s. 6d. net.

IN SEARCH OF ENGLAND

THE CALL OF ENGLAND

IN SEARCH OF SCOTLAND

IN SCOTLAND AGAIN

IN SEARCH OF IRELAND

IN SEARCH OF WALES Each, illustrated, 7s. 6d. net.

NOMA (Seiji)

THE NINE MAGAZINES OF KODAN-SHA : The Autobiography of a Japanese Publisher. Illustrated. 10s. 6d. net.

OMAN (Sir Charles)

THINGS I HAVE SEEN 8s. 6d. net.

A HISTORY OF THE ART OF WAR IN THE MIDDLE AGES, A.D. 378–1485. 2 vols. Illustrated. £1 16s. net.

STUDIES IN THE NAPOLEONIC WARS 8s. 6d. net.

PETRIE (Sir Flinders)

A HISTORY OF EGYPT

In 6 Volumes.

Vol. I. FROM THE 1ST TO THE XVITH DYNASTY 12s. net.

Vol. II. THE XVIITH AND XVIIITH DYNASTIES 9s. net.

Vol. III. XIXTH TO XXXTH DYNASTIES 12s. net.

Vol. IV. EGYPT UNDER THE PTOLEMAIC DYNASTY

By EDWYN BEVAN. 15s. net.

PETRIE (Sir Flinders)—*continued*

Vol. V. EGYPT UNDER ROMAN RULE By J. G. MILNE. 12s. net.

Vol. VI. EGYPT IN THE MIDDLE AGES By S. LANE POOLE. 10s. net.

PHILLIPS (Sir Percival)

FAR VISTAS Illustrated. 12s. 6d. net.

POLITICUS

VISCOUNT GREY OF FALLODON Illustrated. 6s. net.

POLLOCK (William)

THE CREAM OF CRICKET Illustrated. 5s. net.

RAGLAN (Lord)

JOCASTA'S CRIME 6s. net.

THE SCIENCE OF PEACE 3s. 6d. net.

ROBSON (Philip A.)

A MANUAL OF HOCKEY Illustrated. 3s. 6d. net.

SELLAR (W. C.) and YEATMAN (R. J.)

1066 AND ALL THAT

AND NOW ALL THIS

HORSE NONSENSE

Each illustrated by JOHN REYNOLDS. 5s. net.

STEVENSON (R. L.)

THE LETTERS Edited by Sir SIDNEY COLVIN. 4 Vols. Each 6s. net.

STOCK (Vaughan)

THE LIFE OF CHRIST Illustrated. 6s. net.

SURTEES (R. S.)

HANDLEY CROSS

MR. SPONGE'S SPORTING TOUR

ASK MAMMA

MR. FACEY ROMFORD'S HOUNDS

PLAIN OR RINGLETS ?

HILLINGDON HALL Each, illustrated, 7s. 6d. net.

JORROCKS'S JAUNTS AND JOLLITIES

HAWBUCK GRANGE Each, Illustrated, 6s. net.

TAYLOR (A. E.)

PLATO : THE MAN AND HIS WORK £1 1s. net.

PLATO : TIMÆUS AND CRITIAS 6s. net.

ELEMENTS OF METAPHYSICS 12s. 6d. net.

TILDEN (William T.)

THE ART OF LAWN TENNIS Revised Edition.

SINGLES AND DOUBLES Each, Illustrated, 6s. net.

TILESTON (Mary W.)

DAILY STRENGTH FOR DAILY NEEDS
3s. 6d. net.
India Paper.   *Leather*, 6s. net.

UNDERHILL (Evelyn)

MYSTICISM   *Revised Edition.*
15s. net.
THE LIFE OF THE SPIRIT AND THE
LIFE OF TO-DAY   7s. 6d. net.
MAN AND THE SUPERNATURAL
3s. 6d. net.
THE GOLDEN SEQUENCE
Paper boards, 3s. 6d. net ;
Cloth, 5s. net.
MIXED PASTURE : Essays and
Addresses   5s. net.
CONCERNING THE INNER LIFE
2s. net.
THE HOUSE OF THE SOUL   2s. net.

VIEUCHANGE (Michel)

SMARA : THE FORBIDDEN CITY
Illustrated. 8s. 6d. net.

WARD (A. C.)

TWENTIETH CENTURY LITERATURE
5s. net.
THE NINETEEN-TWENTIES 5s. net.
LANDMARKS IN WESTERN LITERA-
TURE   5s. net.
AMERICAN LITERATURE 7s. 6d. net.
WHAT IS THIS LIFE ?   5s. net.
THE FROLIC AND THE GENTLE : A
CENTENARY STUDY OF CHARLES
LAMB   6s. net.

WILDE (Oscar)

LORD ARTHUR SAVILE'S CRIME AND
THE PORTRAIT OF MR. W. H.
6s. 6d. net.
THE DUCHESS OF PADUA
3s. 6d. net.
POEMS   6s. 6d. net.
LADY WINDERMERE'S FAN
6s. 6d. net.
A WOMAN OF NO IMPORTANCE
6s. 6d. net.
AN IDEAL HUSBAND 6s. 6d. net.
THE IMPORTANCE OF BEING EARNEST
6s. 6d. net.
A HOUSE OF POMEGRANATES
6s. 6d. net.
INTENTIONS   6s. 6d. net.
DE PROFUNDIS and PRISON LETTERS
6s. 6d. net.
ESSAYS AND LECTURES 6s. 6d. net.
SALOMÉ, A FLORENTINE TRAGEDY,
and LA SAINTE COURTISANE
2s. 6d. net.
SELECTED PROSE OF OSCAR WILDE
6s. 6d. net.
ART AND DECORATION
6s. 6d. net.
FOR LOVE OF THE KING
5s. net.
VERA, OR THE NIHILISTS
6s. 6d. net.

WILLIAMSON (G. C.)
THE BOOK OF FAMILLE ROSE
Richly illustrated.   £8 8s. net.

WOLFE (Humbert)
THE UNKNOWN GODDESS
PORTRAITS BY INFERENCE
Each 5s. net.

METHUEN'S COMPANIONS TO MODERN STUDIES

SPAIN. E. ALLISON PEERS. 12s. 6d. net.
GERMANY. J. BITHELL. 15s. net.
ITALY. E. G. GARDNER. 12s. 6d. net.
FRANCE. R. L. G. RITCHIE. 12s. 6d. net.

METHUEN'S HISTORY OF MEDIEVAL AND MODERN EUROPE

In 8 Vols. *Each* 16s. net.

I.	476 to 911.	By J. H. BAXTER.
II.	911 to 1198.	By Z. N. BROOKE.
III.	1198 to 1378.	By C. W. PREVITÉ-ORTON.
IV.	1378 to 1494.	By W. T. WAUGH.
V.	1494 to 1610.	By A. J. GRANT.
VI.	1610 to 1715.	By E. R. ADAIR.
VII.	1715 to 1815.	By W. F. REDDAWAY.
VIII.	1815 to 1923.	By Sir J. A. R. MARRIOTT

Methuen & Co. Ltd., 36 Essex Street, London, W.C.2

Hum
PN
1997
P76
1977

DATE DUE

NOV 2 4 1995

SEP 2 6 1996